"This book is a tour de force—an angle on understanding the life of both congregation and pastor that exceeds anything I have ever read. No directions, no programs, just an immersion into what really takes place in the life of a congregation and a pastor. Winn Collier's writing is alive."

Eugene H. Peterson
author of *The Message* and *The Contemplative Pastor*

"This is ultimately a love letter to the church not just for what she can be but for what she already is."

Mandy Smith
pastor, author of *The Vulnerable Pastor: How Human Limitations Empower Our Ministry*

"Shatters all of our idolatrous addictions to big and growing and oversized franchised Christianities. Faithfulness absolutely must become the church's new big. What Collier pens here is nothing short of miraculous. These letters demand to be read."

A. J. Swoboda
pastor, professor, author of *The Dusty Ones: Why Wandering Deepens Your Faith*

"In the venerable epistolary tradition of Saint Paul and François Fénelon, Winn Collier brings us glowing spiritual letters for today, wholehearted meditations on friendship, grief, hope, doubt—and faith in a loving God who is near. *Love Big, Be Well* is a beautiful book for strugglers and seekers, written by a compassionate pastor we come to love."

Karen Wright Marsh
author of *Vintage Saints and Sinners:*
25 Christians Who Transformed My Faith

"*Love Big, Be Well* is a welcome mat, a handwritten invitation, a gigantic wrap-around porch, a warm night filled with fireflies. There may not be a surefire formula for living a wide-open, hope-filled life, but this collection of earnest words comes very close."

Deidra Riggs
author of *Every Little Thing:*
Making a World of Difference Right Where You Are

"Winn Collier places a bundle of letters on our doorstep to remind us 'how to live good lives together in this one place we've been given.' These are truths we know but have sadly forgotten. And we need a good pastor to rouse our memory."

John Blase
author of *The Jubilee* and *Know When to Hold 'Em*

LOVE BIG, BE WELL

Letters to a Small-Town Church

WINN COLLIER

WILLIAM B. EERDMANS PUBLISHING COMPANY

GRAND RAPIDS, MICHIGAN

Wm. B. Eerdmans Publishing Co.
2140 Oak Industrial Drive NE, Grand Rapids, Michigan 49505
www.eerdmans.com

26 25 24 23 22 21 20 19 18 17   2 3 4 5 6 7 8 9 10

ISBN 978-0-8028-7413-9

Library of Congress Cataloging-in-Publication Data

Names: Collier, Winn, 1971– author.
Title: Love big, be well : letters to a small-town church / Winn Collier.
Description: Grand Rapids : Eerdmans Publishing Co., 2017. |
    Includes bibliographical references.
Identifiers: LCCN 2017025198 | ISBN 9780802874139
    (softcover : acid-free paper)
Subjects: LCSH: Clergy—Fiction. | Rural churches—Fiction. |
    Interpersonal relations—Fiction. | GSAFD: Epistolary fiction. |
    Christian fiction.
Classification: LCC PS3603.O452 L69 2017 | DDC 813/.6—dc23
    LC record available at https://lccn.loc.gov/2017025198

The poem "The Peace of Wild Things" by Wendell Berry, which appears in the letter "Sabbaths Everywhere," is from *The Selected Poems of Wendell Berry*, and is reprinted here with the permission of the author. This is a work of fiction. Any resemblance to actual people, places, or events is purely coincidental.

To the good people of All Souls Charlottesville.

Together, we're making beautiful stories.

THE LETTERS

ix

LOVE BIG, BE WELL

AMY'S LETTER

Lent / March 2008

*H*ANK PIERCE AND AMY QUITMAN WERE NEIGH-
*bors on Rural Route 28. Their mailboxes shared a
weathered post at the end of the gravel lane. This seemed
fitting, since their families also shared a weathered pew
at Granby Presbyterian Church. Hank and Amy—along
with Tom, the tire salesman, and Luther, the county's
public defender—made up Granby's Pastoral Search
Committee. Though a thankless job, their assignment
did mean that every Thursday night they'd sit in the
church's empty manse, drink Folgers, and enjoy a few
minutes shooting the bull. Then they'd return to the pile
of resumes that represented the fleeting hope for their
beleaguered flock.*

*This Thursday, though, after the coffee and the gos-
sip, they sat quietly, staring at the stack. Over these last
several months, they'd endured phone interviews with
four candidates and visits from two more. After confirm-
ing the town's modest population or seeing the church's*

humble clapboard building, three candidates quickly exited the process. One candidate turned out to be an ex-con and abruptly stopped answering their calls. Last they heard, he was back preaching in the pen.

Another of the candidates had only been in the room with them ten minutes before commencing his pitch on how necessary it would be to change the church's name. Two leadership books and a weekend conference had convinced him that "Revolution Tribe" would attract folks by the truckload. The final candidate, after an hour of meet-and-greet, pulled out his MacBook to cue up a presentation on the exponential growth curve of satellite campuses. Somehow this aspiring clergy missed the miles of farms and the Blue Ridge tree line as he drove into town.

The process had become a circus show. Now Amy and Hank and Luther and Tom were exhausted. The silence stretched on, and no one had the energy to break it.

"I'm bone-tired of interviews," Amy finally said, as she set her frost-blue mug on the table and reached into her purse. Unfolding a sheet of cream stationery, she continued. "I'd like to just send a letter to our candidates—and make them actually write back. With a pen. And real paper."

Luther leaned forward. "What kind of letter?"

"This kind of letter." And Amy began to read.

Dear Potential Pastor,

Thank you for your interest in Granby Presbyterian Church. We're a pretty vanilla congregation, though we do have enough ornery characters to keep a pastor hopping. If you've got a sense of humor, you're not likely to get bored. We pay as much as we can, though it's never enough. Your job is hard, and we know it. I think you'd find us grateful for your prayers and your sermons—and even more grateful for eating apple fritters with us at the Donut Palace.

We do have a few questions for you. Perhaps we're foolish, but I'm going to assume you love Jesus and aren't too much of a loon when it comes to your creed. We want theology, but we want the kind that will pierce our soul or prompt tears or leave us sitting in a calm silence, the kind that will put us smack-dab in the middle of the story, the kind that will work well with a bit of Billy Collins or Mary Karr now and then. Oh, and we like a good guffaw. I'll be up-front with you: we don't trust a pastor who never laughs. We'll put up with a lot—but that one's a deal-killer.

Here are our questions. We'd like to know if you're going to use us. Will our church be your opportunity to right all the Church's wrongs, the ones you've been jotting down over your vast ten years of experience? (Sorry, I'm one of the ornery ones.) Is our church going to be your opportunity to finally enact that one flaming vision you've had in your crosshairs ever since seminary, that one strategic model that will finally get this Church-thing straight? Or might we hope that our church could be a place where you'd settle in with us and love alongside us, cry with us and curse the darkness with us, and remind us how much God's crazy about us?

In other words, the question we want answered is very simple: Do you actually want to be our pastor?

I'm trying to be as straight as I know how: Will you love us? And will you teach us to love one another? Will you give us God—and all the mystery and possibility that entails? Will you preach with hope and wonder in your heart?

Will you tell us, again and again, about "the love that will not let us go," not ever? Will you believe with us—and for us—that the Kingdom is truer than we know—and that there are no shortcuts? Will you tell us the truth—that the huckster promise of a quick fix or some glitzy church dream is 100 percent BS?

∾

Amy placed the letter on the table. The other three stared at the page, silent. Then, one by one, they took the pen and signed their names.

JONAS'S LETTER

Eastertide / April 2008

*J*ONAS MCANN'S NIGHTSTAND HELD A PILE OF *correspondence from church committees, question-naires and profiles bulging from a manila folder. On top of the folder sat his disheveled pile of current reads: Mark Spragg's* Where Rivers Change Direction, *John Irving's* A Prayer for Owen Meany, *a biography on Harriet Tubman, a leather-bound edition of Karl Barth's prayers, and a slim collection of poetry titled* Freebird *published by inmates from the county jail. Jonas picked up one, usually two, of the books nightly, but he hadn't cracked the folder in weeks.*

Every few months, Jonas would find himself so wea-ried by his days trapped in the cubicle at the insurance company, he'd go on another bender and fire off resumes to churches far and wide. Soon after each outburst Jonas would return to his senses and wonder what insanity had overtaken him. With the resumes, Jonas felt like a faceless name writing to faceless names, pimping his pastoral credentials. The last time he attempted a reply, he got as far as question #3 on the Pastoral Candidate Information Form: What vision do you have for our church? Please list the first five strategic steps you would take in order to implement this vision. *Jonas didn't know this church. He wasn't even sure he'd ever heard of the city. So he didn't have the foggiest clue what these fine souls looked like this morning, much less what they should look like three years from now. And anyway, who was he to possess the word on high about the future of people he didn't even know? Jonas figured he'd learned enough to bluff his way through all the hoops, and some of his pastoral compadres suggested that putting his head down and working the system was exactly what the process required. But he just couldn't do it.*

The entire mess made Jonas want to either take a nap or throw a chair through the wall. But what's a pastor to do when he's got no people to pastor?

Then a letter arrived from a woman named Amy on behalf of Granby Presbyterian. Handwritten. A single page. They didn't drill him with knucklehead questions. They only asked if he was actually interested in being a pastor. The next morning, Jonas rose an hour early to work out his reply.

∾

Dear Amy, Luther, Tom, and Hank,

I can't tell you how good it is to write a letter to actual people with actual names. "To Whom It May Concern" has worn me thin.

I think we're good on the creed. I can't honestly say I always believe all the words, but I pray them anyway. I ask God to help me believe them more. In my experience, anyone who says "we believe" too glibly either hasn't suffered much or simply isn't paying attention. Then again, praying the creed with a little fear and trembling, a gut-hope that it's all true, yields a sturdiness deserving of the word *faith*. At any rate, the creed is necessarily something we say together, something we can only truly believe *together*. So if this candidate process leads anywhere, we'd have to hold one another up. We'd have to keep asking each other whether or not we believe. I assume I'd hold you up on your weak days, and you'd hold me up on mine.

I notice you didn't ask about my family. In a way, that's nice. A previous church thought my wife and I came as a package deal. They were in for a shocker. Alli doesn't play piano. Truthfully, she'd need a bucket to carry a tune. She doesn't do children's ministry, either. And she's never been to a women's ministry craft night or a Christian women's conference. If your heart's broken or you need someone to drop an expletive and pray with you against the evil, Alli's your gal. But she's her own woman, and we like it that way. My wife's a firecracker. She's my truest friend, and the person I respect most in the world. Sometimes I gush about her in sermons, so you'd have to get used to that. She's probably the best Christian I know, but every so often, she'll tell me, "Jonas, I love God, and I love you—but right now I'm barely tolerating Sundays." That admission used to make me nervous. I mean, if the pastor's wife quit the church, it would make for awkward conversations. I don't get nervous anymore, though. Alli listens to God, so what good would my scrambling panic do?

We have two sons and a daughter (Ash, Eli, and Mercy). They have their own faith, but they've got all the issues every kid has. It's tough work being a kid these days. If you expect more from my three than you expect from your own—or if you expect the same but you're all over-achievers who set the bar sky-high—we should probably end this right here.

I have to tell you—reading your letter, you sound fatigued to me. And I find that comforting. I know I'm exhausted. I'm exhausted because of the hours I'm pulling at a job that sucks the life right out of me. I'm exhausted for the same reasons we all are— trying to put food on the table and pay the mortgage and run in four directions at once. But mainly I'm sucking wind because it seems as though I'm wired for a world that doesn't exist anymore.

Initially, I went to seminary because ministry was the family trade, my dad having been a pastor for forty-six years. But I stayed in seminary because of a funeral and a painting. The funeral was for my best friend's 21-month-old daughter. They put her to bed one night, and she never woke up again. I witnessed as the agony broke my friend, shattered his marriage. And all my doubts, all the angst lurking at the fringes for so many years, rushed forward and sunk their talons into my soul. It was my friend's grief, but it became my crisis.

Seven months later, I attended a gallery showing for another friend. Juli had brushed one of her canvases with simple colors, swashes of blues and greens. This painting hung in a side section of the exhibit, and when I turned the corner and caught my first glimpse, my eyes went moist. I still don't know what that moment was about, but I decided then and there that Dostoevsky was right: beauty will save the world. Beauty, which I understand to be another word for *love*, offered the only hope I could imagine for the horror my friends had experienced. It was the only hope for the endless anxieties and labyrinthine questions I carried. I needed love in person, love powerful and alive. I needed beauty to overwhelm all the ugly. As I understood the Bible's story, I needed Jesus.

So I committed my life to walking alongside people who I hoped to call friends. I committed to learning how to help people pray. I determined it would be my job to simply recount, over and again, that one beautiful story of how Love refused to tally the costs but came for us, came to be with us, came to heal us. I took ordination vows and promised that though I might be asked to do many things as pastor, I would always do this one thing: I would point to God. And I would say one simple word: "Love."

But it didn't take me long to figure out that lots of churches don't actually want a pastor. They want a leadership coach or a fundraising executive or a consultant to mastermind a strategic takeover (often performed under the moniker of *evangelism* or *missional engagement*). In this scheme, there's little room for praying and gospel storytelling, for conversations requiring the slow space needed if we're to listen to love. All the things I thought I had been called to do were now ancillary. They barely registered on my job description.

So, after nearly fourteen years, I packed it in. I just couldn't make sense of things anymore. Still, eighteen months ago, I started looking for a church to serve again. I couldn't escape the vows. I had made promises, and so far as I've heard, God hasn't let me loose yet. There's still a fire in my belly. But I have to warn you: I've got zilch energy for playing churchy games. I've got a decent knowledge of who I am and who I'm not. I have a fair idea of what

I've got to say, and who I've got to be. I'll laugh and dance and hope and pray and fight and believe— and I'll ask forgiveness whenever I screw up. But I won't strap on the clerical collar just to play a role. I won't prance about on eggshells trying to keep everyone content with how the machine grinds on time. The truth is, my give-a-shit's broke. I'm not saying this is entirely healthy. God knows, I need salvation as much as the next person. But if you get me, this is what you get.

Too much pastoral leadership literature re-circulates anxious efforts to make the church significant or influential or up-to-date, as if they need to harangue the church into *becoming* some-thing. I think my job is to remind the church that she already *is* something. Can we settle down and be who we are, *where* we are? Can we take joy in the beauty already present in us and around us, right here, as things are? In contradiction to the brassy or the instantaneous, I take my pastoral motto from Mary Oliver, who insists that our spiritual practice doesn't require the lushness of "the blue iris"; all we need is "weeds in a vacant lot, or a few small stones." All we need is to keep watching, keep doing the best we can with what-ever we have.

This letter is too long, just like my sermons. I'm working on it. But all this is to say that if our conver-sation leads anywhere and I were to join your motley band, *being your pastor* is the only thing I'd know how to do. I'm at an utter loss on anything else.

Oh—and one more thing. Aside from the normal financial and vacation considerations (and this would be a good place to say that six weeks of vacation is a bare minimum), I've just now decided that I would insist on one further contractual obligation. If I were your pastor, I'd want to continue this letter-writing thing. We're on to something.

> Love big. Be well.
> *Jonas McAnn*

A LIFE IN GRANBY

Ordinary Time (Pentecost) / October 2008

Dear Friends,

You've shown such kindness to Alli and me, asking how we're settling in and if you can do anything to help. When we arrived in our twenty-six-foot Penske truck (*and God, please never make me get behind the wheel of one of those beasts again*), the group of you standing in the yard, smiling and eager, told us everything we needed to know about whether or not we would be welcome here, whether or not we would find a home at this address. As anyone who's ever walked the marriage aisle will tell you, there's a world of difference between the giddy first date and that terrifying moment when you actually stand across from one another in front of God and all your friends and family, the two of you committing to a life together. I had the jitters as we pulled near town, wondering if we'd made a foolish mistake hauling our family cross-country to a place we didn't know, to live with people we'd met in person only once. When we passed the *Granby: Live a Little* sign, my stomach turned a somersault. *This thing's for real.*

But there you were, and someone had mowed our yard and someone had placed a row of potted herb plants on our front porch. Alli squeezed my hand. That's when we knew our family would be okay.

I understood right off why, when our church's governing body needed a leader, you chose Luther DuBois as clerk. That man does not see chaos; he sees possibility. If Washington, D.C., borrowed him for a few weeks, they'd clean up the environment, bring our soldiers home, expunge the national debt, and lock up the capitol for a long vacation. Guys like me marvel at guys like Luther. As soon as we exchanged hellos, he asked to take a peek inside the truck in order to strategize unloading efforts. After he peeled back the furniture blankets, he surveyed our massive bedroom furniture, the heavy oak pieces that could double as a bomb shelter should the need arise. "Well, they're hefty," he observed.

Next, Luther stepped into the house to formulate his angle of attack, halting at the steep, narrow stairs leading up to where our behemoth furniture needed to land. He craned his neck toward the second floor, calculating. Then he exhaled and shook his head. "Whew." Resting his hands on his hips, he said, "You know, the regional Presbytery hasn't voted on transferring your clergy credentials yet. We could turn that truck back toward Austin and just call this a big misunderstanding." He paused long enough to make me nervous, then broke out in laughter.

Thankfully, Don Brady showed up. He had to duck his head to enter our front door. He shook my hand and pulled me toward him, a minnow swallowed by a whale. With Don on the scene, the furniture arrived upstairs in no time. Later, Ash and I watched wide-eyed when Don asked several fellows to hoist our refrigerator onto his back. He lugged that monstrosity all the way into the kitchen. I tried to stop him, but he blew me off. That was the day our kids started calling Don *Hulk*. Thanks, Don and Luther—thanks, everyone—for such a generous welcome.

As we've begun to get to know one another, I've noticed how some of you are tentative with your questions, as though you're asking one thing but maybe wondering something else. I've heard several self-deprecating quips about Granby's small-town ways, how Alli and I must be twiddling our thumbs and missing Austin's energy. I'm guessing the question not being asked is whether, once the new shine wears off, we will root our lives here. All I can say is that we intend to. I didn't drive that demon truck 1,458 miles to simply drop our gear anywhere. We moved *here*. Granby Presbyterian exists in only one locale: Granby, Virginia. And to belong to this church means to belong to this place. It will take time, but we'd like to make a life here, if you'll have us.

For me, belonging requires a regular haunt with familiar faces and top-shelf coffee. Stu's Mud fits the bill. I was making only my second visit when Stuart Hybe invited me to the back of his shop and showed off his baby, the vintage 12kg Otto Swadlo Roaster that he had restored bolt by bolt. I leaned closer as he described the subtle notes he coaxes from his beans. He rubbed his hand along the roaster's barrel, the way a rancher strokes the neck of his horse. "Swadlo built his roasters in a little storefront in Vienna," Stu explained. "His designs haven't changed since the 1920s. Didn't need to. These Ottos purr like a kitten." While it's important to locate good coffee, it's essential to find good people whose love for their little nook of the world leaves you wanting to love your own little nook better.

You probably already know this, since Amy Quitman belongs to this cadre, but two or three mornings a week, a group of five or six friends faithfully gathers at Stu's. Atop their table sits a laminated card: *Reserved for the Order of the Roasted Bean*. These friends have shared breakfast together for twenty-six years. I've ventured enough questions to learn they've moved from location to location, outlasting business cycles and evolving demographics. They've welcomed spouses and stood together at gravesides. They've laughed together, weathered arguments, shared tears. They are, simply put, friends. One of them told me, "We're a shabby bunch, but we've gotten used to ourselves." I will never belong to this circle, but I can belong to the kind of place where this circle happens. And I can hope to form a circle of my own.

A few weeks ago, I stood in line behind a man who I recognized as a regular member of the Order. This gentleman must have been in his early seventies; he was trim and fit, a real beatnik. Brooks Brothers with a dash of bohemian panache: khakis, Bulgari glasses, and a purple Grateful Dead t-shirt underneath his olive tweed jacket. Most striking, however, was his bushy silver hair flowing to his shoulders. Never, not even in college, have I enjoyed such magnificent hair. When he spoke to the barista, his Dutch accent deepened his intriguing aura. When we moved over to wait for our Americanos, I couldn't help myself. "Maybe this is weird, but I've got to tell you—I'm jealous of your hair."

He chuckled. He'd surely heard this more than once.

"What's the secret?" I asked.

He leaned over to whisper in my ear. "Lots of

sex." Then he patted me on the back and walked off with his double shot.

Stu's. This is a place I'm going to enjoy.

We were drawn to Granby because of a letter Amy, along with the search committee, wrote. The letter was spunky, and it plucked a low chord in me, touched places in me I had forgotten. After all the decisions were made, Amy wrote me another letter. She offered encouraging words; but what struck me most was this: *Just bring us yourself, Jonas. Whatever else pastors might do when they come to a new church, please just bring us yourself.* Of course, in true Amy fashion, she also concluded with a postscript: *To relieve any potential stress, I'm happy to grade your sermons on a curve.* Thank you, Amy. Every little bit helps.

I listened to Amy (something I've discovered is generally a good thing to do). So, here I am. You'll notice, however, that I have not arrived on a white horse. I have not come to fix anything. I have come to pastor, and hopefully to love you; but I also need to be loved as well. Austin offered us many beautiful joys, and I will always be grateful for them. But we endured more than a few dark days there. For a long time, I couldn't speak of this pain; it was too raw to touch. Later, even as dear friends walked with us through those swampy places, it was important to hold our story close—not hiding, but tending to ourselves with care and reverence.

Authenticity is a fine thing, but I'm weary of the ways we blurt out our deepest treasures, creating a kind of relational shock and awe. Our cathartic gushing may be a necessary step in our healing, but it is also a sign we have not yet made peace with ourselves. I believe that in a true friendship, a story arrives whenever it's supposed to. For now, it is enough to say that I don't have the world by the tail. I know what it is to weep and wonder if you will ever be whole again. I know what it is to look in the mirror, to see emptiness staring back, to fear you may have lost your soul. There will be plenty of time for my story, plenty of time for yours.

By now you know that I'm a simple pastor. I don't carry much whiz-bang. I can write letters, though, and I'd like to offer these to you. Letters require time, a listening ear, a curious heart. And I can offer those. I'm aware of Jane Austen's conviction: "Everybody allows that the talent of writing agreeable letters is peculiarly female." Who am I to quibble with Ms. Jane? But I'll give it a go.

I write because I believe there's something deeply human in spacious conversations, something that cannot be duplicated with an email blast. I write because I want to pay attention to the life happening around me, and I want to help you pay attention too. I write because I want to be the kind of person who would linger and write a letter, and because I suspect I have happened upon friends who instinctively know, perhaps better than I do, what I mean.

Love big. Be well.
Jonas

A CHURCH FOR GRANBY

Ordinary Time (Epiphany) / February 2009

Dear Friends,

At our denomination's General Assembly in Boston, we endured hand-wringing over demographic reports and forecasts threatening the demise of religious faith among younger generations. Because I haven't been serving a church for a while, it's been years since I've been to an assembly. I forgot how angst oozes at these things. One of our executives, a tall, fidgety fellow, attempted to conclude his report on an uptick, admonishing us on the power of prayer and the comfort of providence; but it felt like we'd buried the family dog. Perhaps this explains why, when I invited Alli to go to Boston with me, she touched my shoulder and smiled. "I won't be able to do that."

After the Dire Report, Rev. Valerie Hollister stood to give the evening's benediction. I'd heard of Rev. Hollister, a pastor in Harlem for more than forty years. She looked out over us, invoking stillness. When she spoke, her voice resonated like thunder, yet somehow also landed gentle as a feather. Four thousand attendees stretched across the massive hall came to immediate attention at her first slow and deliberate line: *Beloved Children of God . . .* I leaned forward. Like a man catching rain in the desert, I sat poised for every word.

Why do you worry about your life, what you will eat or drink, or about your body, what you will wear? Can one of you by worrying add a single hour to your life? Dear brothers, dear sisters, when we have so much to lose, then the fear of losing any of it terrifies. So let's go ahead and lose, lose it all. Let it burn. Then let's move on to the joy. It is our birthright to live as joyful children sustained by the kindness and mercy of our Father. Do not fret. Give way to the grace of losing your life. We are God's dear children. And we will be okay. Amen.

Then Rev. Hollister made the sign of the cross over us. And one more time, she said, *You are God's dear children.* I would drive to Boston again to receive that blessing.

For those of us gathered at the assembly, I suspect our pessimism centers on the imminent shrinkage of infrastructure, budgets, and pensions. Of course, I prefer that my paycheck continue to arrive on the 15th and 30th of each month, but I find it difficult to get exercised over all this. I recall Jesus once saying something about the necessity of going the way of the seed: that we must eventually fall into the ground, cold and dead, before resurrection could ever happen.

Whatever the future may bring, we'll welcome what comes. The constant suggestion in Boston was that we needed to overhaul our identity to appeal to the escalating number of those who "like Jesus but not the church." I get this. Almost every time I see a Christian spokesperson on CNN, I pray to God the producers misidentify him or her as a financial guru, a Civil War re-enactor, a Martian— anything but a Christian. Where do they find these people? If I had a genie, I'd use my three wishes to secure a muzzle for every boisterous Christian whenever there was (1) an election, (2) a legal ruling on the intersection of civil rights and sexuality, or (3) any tragedy or natural disaster.

Don Brady told me about the time several years back when he was first circling around our church, wary of us even while intrigued. He told me how he remembered saying to Amy Quitman, "You folks seem nice, and I like most of you. But religious people make me nervous."

"Me too," Amy answered. "And I'm even one of

them." Don laughed. "Unfortunately," Amy added, "if you're looking for people to disappoint you, we will provide the material. In spades."

When religious experts suggest an identity update, the whole proposal amounts, in my book, to nothing more than a grand slogan and a fresh coat of paint. We could try to re-envision ourselves as a community center or a social advocacy firm if we want to wrench ourselves trying to fit into someone else's clothes. But look, we *are* the church. We're incompetent at most endeavors, but the Spirit has gifted us with divine energy to live into a simple and straightforward vocation. Gathered at Jesus's table, we feast on true life and then disperse into our run-of-the-mill lives as witnesses to the Kingdom of this Jesus who loves the whole world. The world needs *more* of who we are, not less.

Our entire story is predicated on the assumption that we're massive screw-ups. What's supposed to be unique to Christians is how we're the first to recognize the trouble we're in, the first to cry uncle. If we want to lead in anything, it's this prayer: *Help me. I've made a mess of things.*

And boy, how often have we made a mess of things. We've screwed up more than a few of the basics: neglecting care for the poor and the children, failing to nurture creation, participating in systems of power rather than sacrificially laying down our power for others. And yet this is why we need the church all the more. This is not the time to surrender the whole idea of church, nor is it the time to retreat into empty theological ideals or rhetoric that have nothing to do with our place and our neighbors. We don't need religious platitudes. We need an actual community devoted to our home, to Granby. We need a community of friends who take on responsibility for Granby, who will suffer alongside it and refuse to lose hope in it. Some moments require a people who will stand up and say, *In this moment, this is how the love of Christ compels us. . . .* The only thing worse than our failing to inhabit mercy and holiness would be our making no attempt at all, our fading into our own isolated lives, where we are each left to our own whims and proclivities.

I am responsible for meeting you at the Eucharist table, whether I like you or not. And you are responsible for meeting me. We are commanded to love one another, and together, to love our neighbors. We have pledged fidelity to Jesus Christ, and we have renounced all other gods and idols. These facts carry tangible implications for our lives, and we are responsible for living into these obligations together. We couldn't possibly do it alone. The Scriptures are not merely stories of individuals— they're stories of communities. And God's Spirit animates us. We are not, finally, a community of our own making.

The Scriptures refer to the church as a *family*, not an *institution*. Those of us who (either because of exhaustion or exasperation) refuse any responsibility to the broader community of faith might think *family* frames an über-local, organic paradigm that relieves us of these complicated burdens with the church-at-large. But *family* really only binds our cords tighter. Have you ever had an aging parent or a difficult sibling? Have you ever felt the weight of responsibility for your family reputation or your heritage? Have you ever had children?

Earlier I mentioned Valerie Hollister's blessing. I return to it regularly. When you have a moment, sit in a quiet place and hear her words again. We really are going to be okay.

Love big. Be well.
Jonas

THE GROUND OF LOVE

Eastertide / May 2009

Dear Friends,

Yesterday, on my walk up Three Sisters Mountain, I happened upon a fledgling bluebird that had apparently tumbled out of her nest too soon. The poor creature flapped and rolled in the dirt, frantic but determined. I feared if I intervened, my lingering scent would likely result in the chick being abandoned. So I stepped away quietly and sat down to watch. Within a few minutes, the momma swooped down, dropped a morsel in the agitated chick's mouth, chirped some motherly instruction, and then flew above the trees, circling. The grounded chick flapped with new fury but managed only to kick up a small cloud of dust. Eventually the momma landed again, offered another bit of food, and then flew away, just as before. This became the routine: momma flying like a sentinel, landing, feeding, then returning above where she could keep watch. She did this over and again.

Eventually, I walked on. I don't know the fledgling's fate, but I do know that momma blue did all she could manage. She couldn't return her chick to safety. She could only circle near, watch with care, and offer the best she had to give, no matter how meager. So she stayed close and hoped favor would bend their way. I think this is how it is for most of us who love someone or carry concern for this world. We will never be able to right all wrongs or heal every wound. We cannot keep harm from those dearest to us. To love is to do our best and then to hope, to have faith. Often, love means simply circling and staying near—trusting that this will somehow prove enough.

Above all else, we must ground ourselves in love—that's what Saint Paul wrote. Not what you'd expect to hear from Paul, is it, this apostle who trimmed doctrinal imprecision like a butcher trims the fat? Love, Paul believed, keeps us at the center, very near to God. This kind of love has little in common with doe-eyed banalities. Real love sometimes manifests a fierce strength. Love restrains us when we're running toward ruin. Love will be firm or gentle, whichever is necessary. Love also assumes we are frail, flawed creatures who often limp through confusion and temptation as best we're able.

I once heard a good teacher say, "God is too busy delighting in us to be disappointed in us." I'm still pondering what I think about this. On the one hand, when God endures our vitriol and violence, the ways we heap shame on each other, how we use God's name to enact (or cover) pure evil—surely God feels something like disappointment, maybe even grief. And yet doesn't the story we cling to tell us how God's love refuses to be extinguished, ever?

Don Brady told me that on his road toward faith, all the bells and whistles went off for him during yet another conversation with Amy. (Apparently they had quite a few of these talks.) You may remember this from one of the times Don has shared bits of his story. Amy stopped by Tom Felton's Garage to have new tires mounted, and Don happened to be there with his red Kawasaki Voyager up on the lift, tinkering with his two-wheeled baby and irritating Tom, as he loves to do. When Tom had to take a phone call, Don saw Amy alone in the customer lounge and joined her. Eternal questions must have been sitting right near the surface for him, because they were barely past hellos before they found themselves in deep waters. Don has been candid with all of us about his past—his rough marriages, his estrangement from his daughter. "I know what you folks say about God's love covering everything," he told Amy. "It would have to be a big, big love for me."

31

Amy nudged closer to Don and put her arm around his shoulders, as far as she could stretch. And then she just sat there, quiet. Don told me he looked around nervously, certain everyone was watching, and he remembers Julio Iglesias crooning "Mona Lisa" over the speaker system. "I felt awkward," Don said, "but I also felt something else. I think I'd call it joy."

Amy sat for a while longer before speaking. Finally she said, "It's big, Don. The love is really big."

When we think about the Apostle Paul's instruction to ground ourselves in love, I take the word *ground* literally. The Psalmist insists that the earth is full of God's unfailing love. This means the dirt on which we walk, the very ground holding us up every day of our lives, pulses with God's love. And it makes no difference whether we welcome God's kindness or mock the whole idea. Love holds us. Love will never leave. Love is big.

We may construct rigid confines, but love's always at play, tiptoeing past our boundaries, dancing in a foreign country. Love may bind our wounds, or love may press into our pain. Either way, we have little say in the matter. Love will hold us until the end.

I've had an odd dream recur two or three times. I walk into an elegant party, plush with Hugo Boss and Ralph Lauren models, beautiful people holding champagne glasses close to their chest and whispering into one another's ear. Except I realize I'm buck-naked. Laughter fills the room as I stand there, knees pressed together, hands stretched down to cover me as I back my way out the door. Please tell me you've had dreams like this too. . . .

I'm no Carl Jung, but it seems obvious to me I carry some dread that I'll be found out, uncovered as a fraud, not the man you think I am, the competent pastor you may believe me to be. Perhaps my wife will learn the depth of my insecurities, or my kids will discover I'm winging this whole parent thing. But whenever I'm under the sway of my self-obsession or inner terror, I eventually find myself near one of you. Without you knowing it (and in your own unique way), you pull me back toward the truth. Like Amy, you put your arm around me. You say a kind word. You ask a thoughtful question. You get me to laugh. You carry me back into the truer story. Love really is big.

Often, the best we can do is show up for one another, trusting love's firm ground to hold true. Sometimes, like that momma bluebird, all we can do is circle and watch and stay close. And in the end, it will be enough.

Love big. Be well.
Jonas

ST. JAMES'S MANTRA

Ordinary Time (Pentecost) / June 2009

Dear Friends,

Every age has its unique way of wrestling with the same predictable temptations. I don't give much credence to the thundering doomsayers who bellow about our generation's alarming monopoly on greed, violence, and lewdness. We make the same blunders as those before us, only now we make them faster—and maybe with more hubris.

But maybe each generation wrestles more acutely with one particular sin. To riff on Saint Paul, the sin that does so easily beset us might be noise. And I don't just mean that we need more contemplation and solitude. I mean we just talk too much.

Recently Luther DuBois told me a great story about the summer he visited his Grandma Looma in Atlanta. One of Looma's neighbors, Ms. Ida, stopped by one noontime, and Luther was at the kitchen table eating a sandwich. When Ms. Ida entered the room, Luther instinctively cupped his hand to his nose. She arrived in a cloud of vinegar and old onions, doused with a generous dose of lilac perfume. As if this olfactory offense were not enough, Ms. Ida, after placing a warm pound cake on the counter, stepped closer and hugged Luther, pressing his nose into her bosom. "Ewww!" he exclaimed. "What's that smell?" In an instant, Looma grabbed a roll of skin underneath Luther's arm and twisted so hard that water flooded his eyes. Then she made Luther apologize and exiled him to the porch. After Ms. Ida left, Looma called him back into the kitchen. She tapped him on the forehead and said, "Hon, you don't need to spill out every little pebble that's rolling around in there."

Looma's advice still applies.

Of course, we could also heed the apostle James, who gave us sound wisdom: *Everyone should be quick to listen, slow to speak, slow to get angry*—a mantra appropriate for us. And if an appeal to patience or quiet (or even a little subtlety, for crying out loud) doesn't compel us, how about the simple call to be truthful? I know many of us have vigorous political beliefs and Christian convictions, but so far as I know, this doesn't nullify the Scriptures' demand that we not slander or gossip or invent outrageous stories about whatever politician or religious thinker we dislike. And please, can we stop acting like God's on our side, whatever our side happens to be? I suspect that God would be more liberal than the liberals and more conservative than the conservatives and would tell us all that we're way out of line. We're to do the best we can, in an imperfect world and with the limited wisdom we have—and we're to assume that our neighbors are doing the best they can too. It would probably be prudent if we'd all pipe down. Maybe we could even offer a prayer to God to help us be good people and make good decisions when things get so dang confusing.

I think many of us find it difficult to just sit in our space, to be where we are, to make peace with the contradictions or uncertainties. Social media has given us the unfortunate opportunity to announce our opinions incessantly, to blurt out every passing reaction. But, God help us, we really don't need to spill out every pebble that's rolling around in our heads.

The deep places in our soul, the ambiguous terrain and those areas where we're experiencing seismic shifts, require space and quiet for us to honor what's happening in and *to* us. We need time to consider what our questions uncover and what our experiences mean—and what we are to do with all of this. We need enough distance to discern what is true for us and to discover what may prove in the end to merely be our year of indecision or funk, maybe our knuckle-headed detour.

With all this, I'm really preaching to myself—I know there have been times when I've leveraged my angst to say something edgy, to feel the satisfaction of being irreverent. I enjoy the thrill of gaining others' attention. About a month ago, Alli told me that in my sermon that Sunday I was trying too hard for shock value. And God knows I'm quick to offer my point of view when I think I'm right. But maybe we can step back from the microphone (me first of all) and let our opinions take a backseat to our friendships. Maybe we can actually *live* where we are instead of *telling* everyone where we are.

Last week, when the Pierces and the Quitmans invited all of us over for BBQ, I noticed how so many of us lingered late. There were plenty of drinks in the ice buckets, and Dillon (Amy's son) and his band played into the wee hours. The cool breeze and the bright moon made for an enchanting evening. But what kept us there was each other. We were listening to one another, and we were laughing. And sometimes we were just sitting quietly—but quietly *together*. We need more moments like this. New and old friends, together, on the porch in the evening light.

Love big. Be well.
Jonas

P.S. Even though I'm making a case for reining in our compulsive noise, I'm not suggesting we all bottle up our emotions and play nice. I know there are times when we just need someone to listen while we defuse our anger or anxiety. As the Psalms and the prophets show us, there's a place— and among friends is exactly the right place—for lowering our filters and letting things loose.

CHISELING STONE

Ordinary Time (Pentecost) / September 2009

Dear Friends,

We've reached our first milestone: our first year together. We've gotten to know each other a bit, and we've moved past the pleasantries and into the grit of life. I'm thankful for that. I've never done well at parties where I'm supposed to smile agreeably and make small talk and pretend that taking only two or three of those miniscule hors d'oeuvres curbs my hunger. On these occasions everyone nods in unison and laughs on cue and nibbles their cracker or morsel of cheese, and all the while some of us are thinking, *Good God, would you please stop yammering so I could go get a cheeseburger?*

When our family lived in Austin, we attended one of those upper-crusty civic affairs, a benefit for the University of Texas's art program. Christian Dior tuxes and Emilio Pucci gowns. I assume I was the only one sporting a rental. Every year one of the museum's benefactors fills two tables with guests; that year she generously invited me as the representative member of the clergy—in fact, she invited the entire McAnn family to the gala. Thinking the occasion would provide a cultural experience for the kids where they could practice proper etiquette and get a taste of the fine life, I said yes. But once folks understood I was the one tasked with the evening's benediction, I spent the rest of the night being referred to as *Reverend* and on the receiving end of quick smiles in passing. I also spent a fair bit of my time running interference with Ash and Eli as they attempted to sneak table to table and fill their pockets from the numerous bowls of gourmet chocolate mints. That night, I caught up on lots of high-society protocol, but not a single person asked me my first name.

That evening sits in direct contrast to the time when, several months ago, Luther invited our family to Washington, D.C., for a day trip. Luther had to be at Federal Court for a matter concerning one of his trials, and he invited us to meet him and his family for dinner. He wanted to take us to the swanky *La Casa Viña* in D.C.'s Columbia Heights. After parking at one of the outlying metro stations, we rode the Yellow train into the city. When we arrived at the restaurant, we entered through massive bronze doors and met a *maître d'* with an exotic accent and a red carnation ablaze against his black pinstripe suit.

We walked through a sea of white linen, with flames shooting up from the grill in the open kitchen. Apparently the ambiance bedazzled Luther and Glynna's youngest son, Jay, as much as it did me, because when he jetted off to the restroom, he blew past the signage on the doors. Later Jay told us that he didn't realize his mistake until he sat perched on the toilet and heard women's voices from the bathroom lounge. When he peeked under the stall door, he saw a line of women in fancy dresses dabbing at their faces in front of gold-framed mirrors. (For being only seven, I told Jay later, he kept his cool like a pro.) He crouched in his cube for at least twenty minutes while women flowed in and out. Meanwhile, we began to wonder if Jay was okay, so Luther went to the men's room, only to return empty-handed. Then Glynna went searching and led Jay, beet-red, back to the table.

When we exited the restaurant, the *maître d'* gave Jay a wink. "Next time, you must try the other bathroom. It is also nice." I wouldn't be telling you this story if Jay minded (and at that age our boys would never have allowed me to share the tale), but Jay rode home with us afterwards, and we laughed about it most of the way back. That night, like so many nights with so many of you over the past year, we shared something intimate and true.

At any rate, as you've welcomed our family into your family, I'm thankful we haven't spent much time with formalities and pretense. We've gotten right down to the real—to the living. The Psalmist tells us our days are numbered, and if that's the case, why waste a moment posturing? Dive right in—that's what we've done. Thank you. That's a great kindness.

Let me share a bit of my own story. I come from a long line of pastors. Going back at least five generations, McAnn men—and a few of the women too—have worn the stole. Of course, you'd also find lawyers and electricians and whiskey runners, even one uncle who dodged the IRS for nearly two decades. But our family history holds a thread of preachers. I'm proud of this heritage, the call to live with people, to pray with them and ponder Scripture with them. I believe I'm safe-keeping something sacred handed from one generation to the next. I don't have any expectations that Mercy or Ash or Eli will carry the torch forward, but a father can hope. A father can always hope.

Eli is the namesake of my grandfather, the original Eli McAnn. Eli served a small, poor parish in Pennsylvania, and because they couldn't pay his full salary, Paps honed his craft as a stonemason. Paps Eli built the home where he and his wife, Gigi, lived and died. Every summer, Paps would take me to the quarry where they extracted the rock, and bring me into his shop where he chiseled and worked the stones to size. Several times he took me to some of the places where he had fitted his stones, one atop the other, raising a family's house or a church, once a barn for the horses owned by one of the wealthiest men in the state.

"Every stone has to be cut to size, Jonas," he explained. "Builders sometimes want to rush in with pre-cut materials. That won't do with rock like this." Of course, those other builders made a lot more money than Paps. Given his attention to detail, he could only finish two or three projects a year. "But I'm always grateful for the beauty of them when I'm finished," he told me. "You can't put a price on that." Whenever he laid the final stone on any project, I remember him staring at his work intently. I think what Paps felt was deep contentment, genuine pleasure in how he'd fitted stones to this exact land, how these stones would still be standing long after he was six feet under.

For Paps, being a stonemason and being a pastor were mostly the same kind of work. He wasn't a pre-fab builder, and he wasn't a pre-fab pastor dealing with an assembly-line people. He listened to the land and to the stories, fitting one stone at a time, one life at a time.

This is how I understand my life here, with you;

and I'm grateful. From that first letter I received from Amy, Hank, Luther, and Tom, I've felt your warm invitation. Since then, you've extended that invitation—into your hopes and your heartaches, your celebrations and your sorrows. You've welcomed our family into the fold, though I know you're only able to offer an initial entrance into this community's rich history. You've entrusted me with this place among you, but I know I must show myself trustworthy and earn the deeper belonging, the deeper bond. I received the title *pastor* after a vote, but I will only actually *become* your pastor after years of laying sturdy stone upon sturdy stone. This is the way it's supposed to be. This is work worthy of a life.

In Per Petterson's novel *Out Stealing Horses*, the solitary character Trond reflects some of what I'm trying to say here, in his description of why he's committed himself to building his own cabin:

> *I try to do most of the work myself, even though I could have paid a carpenter. I am far from skint, but then it would have gone too fast. I want to use the time it takes. Time is important to me now, I tell myself. Not that it should pass quickly or slowly, but be only time, be something I live inside and fill with physical things and activities that I can divide it up by, so that it grows distinct to me and does not vanish when I am not looking.*

The lives we live together do not merely serve some cosmic cause. The living of our lives, the chiseling of beautiful stones, *is* the cause. This must have been what the apostle Peter meant when he told us that we are each a living stone. And we cannot simply toss stones together. We must work and watch for a proper fitting. We must trim and smooth the stones and lay them at the angles that this single plot of land demands. We must listen to one another, learning where to be silent and where to speak.

Each of your lives is magnificent and beautiful. Tom and Margie and Hank and Sylvie—you are stunning, chiseled stones. Abel and Misty, Renton and JD—you possess a particular light only you can shine. I want to name each of you here; you are all such singular gifts. I want to help you unearth that one life you must live, and I need you to help me discover mine. We want lives that stand strong and shimmer. We want our time to be as Trond described it, filled with those things necessary for the gritty act of living, which will mark our time as meaningful. We want lives distinct to each of us, solid lives that matter to this world and to our neighbors.

Love big. Be well.
Jonas

DRY BONES

Christmastide / January 2010

Dear Friends,

Well, Old Man Winter has arrived with an attitude. I hope the joy of Christmas lingers for you. The night of mulled cider and pie and caroling hosted by Luther and Glynna DuBois was just the best time. But I don't ever want to see Don in a reindeer suit again.

I recently finished a biography of Harry Truman, and he exclaimed, in a moment of exasperation, "Why is it only sons of bitches who know how to lick a stamp?" I truly hope this isn't how you feel whenever these envelopes and long letters hit your mailbox.

I write for many reasons. Part of it is simply that I appreciate the leisurely pace of writing, and I like the idea of you making time for a leisurely pace for reading. A sermon offers one way of conversing. Meals and coffees and walks in the woods offer another. And letters, still another. I'm looking for every possible way to keep the conversation going.

When I was interviewing with the search committee, Hank told me that a group of you had gone to hear Marilynne Robinson speak in Charlottesville. He explained how Marilynne shared her belief that "when a sermon is preached as one profoundly thoughtful person trying to speak in good faith to other people who are trying very hard to listen in good faith—I think that's one of the more beautiful things that happen in the world." I know this quote exactly because later I asked Hank to repeat it so I could write it down. He asked what I thought about Marilynne's ideas, and I told him I wished I'd been at that event by myself—then I could have plagiarized her in my next month of sermons without anyone knowing. He grinned. "I thought you'd like her."

After a recent Sunday sermon, Morgan Preston said something to me that I haven't been able to shake: "I've always thought sermons were supposed to clarify things, but your sermons usually raise a whole new slew of questions." I asked Morgan what new question he had that morning. "Well," he answered, "you were preaching on Jacob wrestling the Almighty, and I realized that Jacob wrestled God—*God*—to basically a draw. Now how's that possible? How's that gonna work? God's stronger than everything, right?" I told him he'd landed on a puzzler indeed, and I asked him how he felt about grappling with so many questions. "Oh, I don't like it much. I think religion should pony up some answers, but there's something about that wrestling I do want to chew on." After that conversation, I can only say: me too.

If I ever preach a sermon recounting the story of Abraham with his furious tears and his trembling knife raised over dear Isaac, if I tell you such stories and I have no quietness in me, no hint of confusion or reverence, then trust your intuition that something's not right. I may be handing you the facts, but I'm missing the wonder. If I ever preach a sermon on Mary's tears or Judas's betrayal or Jesus's words on the Mount or Jesus's words from the cross—if I ever preach these things without any quiver in my voice or without a struggle to find language for these mysteries, then you'll know that though I may have delivered a sermon, I have not offered you God.

This makes me think of one of those biblical scenes that only God or Tim Burton could have dreamed up. God gave Ezekiel the vision of a wide valley filled knee-deep with bones, brittle corpses picked clean by the vultures and bleached white by the sun. Deader than dead. Then God queried Ezekiel: "Mortal," (and don't you love how God likes to make certain we're clear on who's who) "what do you think—could these bones live again?" Ezekiel, who must have been having quite the day, managed to spit out the only sane response. "How could I possibly say? Only you know answers like that."

Well, that's all I've got. Who can say? Only God knows. . . . Maybe I should incorporate this line into my benediction more often. One of the things I love about our liturgy is how, after the sermon each Sunday, whoever's preaching just stands there, or sits down, and we have a minute or two of silence. Mostly it's uncomfortable, and—let's be honest—with all the kids, the silence isn't all that silent. I'm also aware that a few of you have petitioned to dispense with this practice. But in those few minutes, our words stop, our efforts to make things happen or figure things out stop. Isn't it strange how, in church, where things are supposed to be about God and not about us, it still feels like an odd place to halt our activity and just sit in the mercy of God?

Not long ago, I visited Sylvie Braxton in her studio, admiring several of her recent pieces. (Two of them are heading to a studio in Santa Fe, by the way—you should ask to see them before they're gone.) We sat in her leather chairs, surrounded by so much color, so much life and beauty. I asked Sylvie about her art and how she arrived at her craft. "I just ran out of words," she answered. "I felt I had something to give, but I had absolutely nothing to say. Dry as a bone."

Maybe we have too many words, or the wrong kind of words—ones that push or prod or attack or flatten. Maybe so many shrill, anxious words dry up all the flesh, all the life. I know too many of my sermons scrape away all the playfulness and imagination inherent in a biblical story. Intending to give clarity, instead I strip away all the mystery, leaving nothing but a carcass text and a skeleton congregation. I want to do better than that.

Understanding Sylvie's disposition, I wasn't surprised when she told me her favorite part of our worship was those two silent minutes after the sermon. "It's the moment I feel God most present to me, and me most present to everyone else." To be honest, I was also bothered by her comment at the time. Was my sermon so dispensable? Were our music and Scripture reading and prayers and the Eucharist so unremarkable? But now I understand what Sylvie meant. If we have no quiet, no moment where our proclamations and conclusions and energies cease, then we really have no room for God. Our mouths and our minds, at some point, must stop their clamoring so that we remember that Scripture and the Eucharist, our blessings and prayers arrive as pure gift.

In worship, if we are never bewildered, terrified, or left speechless and silent, if our minds never wobble under the weight of some great mystery, then we've dismissed God from the picture.

This is a tricky business, though. It's not as if God is the great quizmaster and the Bible merely a book of inscrutable riddles leaving us to throw up our hands in resignation and return to scrolling through Facebook. Jesus had more than a few definitive things to say, and his Scriptures don't shy away from speaking a clear and outrageous word.

Some of you know that a small group of us gather for books and coffee and sometimes a little bourbon at Stu's Mud. The group has a highly nuanced name: Words & Beverages. It's a few folks from the Order of the Roasted Bean, a few folks from church, and a few stragglers. Not everything we read is religious, but we've been working through a series of letters between Thomas Merton and Evelyn Waugh, author of *Brideshead Revisited* and Merton's UK editor for *The Seven Storey Mountain*. In one of his letters, Waugh shared his friend Robert Knox's conviction that God was disinterested in literary quality and precision. Merton objected to that idea: "I don't agree with Mgr. Knox that God isn't interested in good prose. I don't think that Our Lord is very pleased with preachers and writers who do their best to get the Church all mixed up." Perhaps we appeal to mystery too easily, a sleight of hand to camouflage every difficult or uncomfortable truth. You may have picked up on how we pastors sometimes like to be confusing because we think it adds to our aura of sophistication. Sometimes we leave things murky because it seems easier than dealing truthfully with God or ourselves or one another.

But sometimes uncertainties and questions persist because we simply don't know what to say—and to say much at all would be a lie. There's more to all this, of course. Maybe you should join us at Stu's and help us mull it over.

Love big. Be well.
Jonas

P.S. One more thought. I had to come back and add this because my mind kept fiddling with Ezekiel. When Ezekiel went to preach his sermon to those bleached bones, he declared, "This is what the LORD God says to you bones—*Live*." And suddenly there was a noise, "a rattling." Those bones moved awkwardly at first, loose and rickety. You'll remember, maybe from the Sunday school song, that the toe bones are connected to the foot bones and the foot bones to the ankle bones, all the way up to the head bone. And Ezekiel's command set those connections in motion: those bones pulled themselves together, dusted off the dirt, and danced. What a crazy sight. A preacher could spend his whole life running on the fumes from an altar call like that. "I will put my Spirit within you," God said. "And you will live." I'm thinking that's what we're really getting after—*life*. Maybe what we're longing for is both words and silence that lead us to life. Maybe that's it.

A MUTT KIND OF LOVE

Lent / March 2010

Dear Friends,

You may have already heard that my wife and kids finally wore me down. Ever since Duke, our Irish Setter, died, I've resisted bringing another dog into the family. It seemed unfaithful to have any other dog tag along as I traipse through the woods.

Aside from his sly, gluttonous fetish for trash, Duke was pretty close to the perfect canine. With one slight whistle from me, he would heel, sticking to my left leg as though we were magnetically attached. And he was attached to all of us. When Mercy was younger, she scared us when she came down with a serious bout of pneumonia. Duke lay beside her bed, day and night, for nearly three weeks. He wouldn't budge until Mercy was no longer bedridden. We still miss him terribly.

Several months ago, though, our neighbor's

et hound, Ginny, had a string of midnight rendezvous and developed a swelling belly to show for her trysts. When the litter arrived, these squealing furballs were luck-of-the-draw mutts, but they were cute little stinkers, so my family ignored my protests and arranged a visit. Alli and the kids set their hearts on the runt of the crew, this pint-sized, dirty-white pup with brown splotches. The little guy was tiny, but he sported an oversized pair of floppy ears. When he tried to wedge his way through the brood and lock onto a nipple, he didn't get further than neck-deep into the hungry pack. His siblings, slurping greedily, squeezed him out. Undeterred, he gathered steam and charged back into the fray, nose first, only to be pushed out again. We watched his valiant, futile efforts for several minutes. The pup was small, but he had spunk. We named him Samson.

Since that day, I've thought more about why we brought Samson home. I believe it's because once we loved Duke, this love made our hearts larger. And once this love exists, it never leaves and still longs to be given away. A sign of an authentic encounter with love is this: we are made larger. Conversely, whenever we spurn love—whenever we fixate on ourselves or grasp after our life or hoard our energy—we are made smaller. We may think that by circling the wagons and closing ourselves off from responsibility to others, we'll preserve our precious life. The truth is that with our life and our love, it's another miracle of loaves and fishes. When we live with open hearts, we make more room for love, and we discover there's plenty. Plenty for us, plenty for everyone else.

Sadly, too often the church hoards love. Committed to the truths of Jesus (a commitment I share), we mistakenly believe this to mean we should fix a vice-grip on our theology, ever vigilant to mark precisely who's in and who's out. While Jesus playfully tinkered with religious dogmas and instigated theological vertigo with his strange teachings, we compulsively codify absolutist and unimaginative explanations for every kind of mystery. We forget how to listen, and we abandon the expansive conversations Jesus engendered. When we insist on precision at the expense of love, we grow smaller.

A few months ago, Don Brady was our Sunday greeter, shaking hands as folks exited church. But Don takes joy in sending people out the door every week. As you know, he stands in the narthex, kissing the babies and the matronly women, sneaking candy to the kids, and dishing out hugs to anyone who will receive them. Is there a better sight than watching this big hunk of a man stooping down and enfolding another person in his massive arms? "Thanks for coming. You're something special." I swear I've heard those words a hundred times, but they still seem fresh to me.

On this particular Sunday, I had repeated Jesus's words about the centrality of love and observed how sad it is whenever Christians turn out to be the meanest folks in town. A middle-aged man was visiting, and he grew visibly irritated. He shook his head and leafed aggressively through his Bible. Before the doxology's final note settled, he hurried, head down, toward the parking lot. The flustered man moved so quickly that he missed Don at the back door, but Don would have none of that. He told me how he caught up to the fellow at his car and thanked him for joining us.

The man fiddled with his keys in the door of his Honda, offering a gruff "Thanks" in reply.

"We'd love to have you again sometime," Don said, making a second pass.

"Not likely." The man opened his door and tossed his jacket onto the passenger seat.

"Are you all right?" Don asked. He is nothing if not persistent.

The man was *not* all right. For the next ten minutes, this serious-minded fellow unleashed a theological discourse that had obviously been corked and building pressure for the past hour. He quoted Calvin and Augustine and Spurgeon. The man was frustrated with soppy churches and squeamish pastors who go lite on wrath.

Don was unfamiliar with most of these arguments. He simply listened, allowing the steam to dissipate. The exasperated man paused for breath, then concluded: "So, a lot of the Bible you've got to explain. Can you really say *love* holds everything else in place?"

Don considered this question, telling me later how he felt in over his head but also how he wanted to honor the fellow's concerns. The parking lot was nearly empty, and quiet. Don answered carefully. "Yep, I think that's the meat of it. Love's the main deal."

There's no reason to pit God's love against God's holiness. That's like trying to slice a heart in two and pretend the thing could keep on beating. God's holiness, terrifying as it may be, offers us a tremendous gift. God's holiness assures us that God's love is pure, trustworthy, untainted by human selfishness or vanity. And our most basic beliefs insist that in all of God's actions toward creation, God's motivation is *love*. The first truth my parents taught me was this: *For God so loved the world. . . .*

I've preached a truckload of sermons on these topics, and darn it if Don Brady, standing in an empty parking lot, didn't nail it better than I ever have. It's love. Love's the main deal.

> Love big. Be well.
> *Jonas*

THE FIRE BRIGADE

Eastertide / May 2010

Dear Friends,

Every so often, someone asks me why I haven't spoken up in a public way about a particular social, political, or theological firestorm. Last year, there was one issue—and honestly, at the moment I don't even remember what it was—that got under Amy's skin. But I do remember her being more than a little perturbed when she asked me, "You *do* have a backbone, don't you?" We both went home tense, but that night she called. "I just get passionate about things sometimes—you know that, right?" We need Amy's passion; it makes us better.

I'll admit it's possible that my silence does demonstrate weakness. I don't relish the fact that some questions leave me no way to navigate any path that wouldn't anger some portion of our community. And there are days when I feel like one of those Texas armadillos attempting a midnight crawl across the rural highway, blinded in a flash of headlights from both directions. I don't like to disappoint you or to feel the sting of your anger.

I've known a few pastors always licking their chops for a fight. I once heard a pastor recount to a group of other pastors how he had delivered an ultimatum to his church board, and how three-fourths of them had resigned en masse. "And you know what?" he said. I remember his wide, white eyes, as though he would come unglued if he couldn't deliver the punch line. "That night, I slept like a baby." He sat back in his chair, satisfied, like a cat after a pounce. There are a hundred reasons why this story disturbs me, but needless to say, I don't have such a disposition. I would *not* sleep like a baby.

Maybe my fear of blowback influences me more than I care to admit. But, as best I know, timidity isn't the heart of the matter for me. I don't always jump into the fray on every question that seems so pressing, so essential, so monumental and imme-diate, because, frankly, I'm suspicious. Whenever wildfire erupts, whenever opinions and editorials and conferences and petitions and books explode like sparks set to parched kindling, I'm suspicious. I refuse to pour gas on the flames. I'd rather join the fire brigade. Whenever any monolithic group (from the right or the left) provokes fear or agi-tates guilt, I'm suspicious. Whenever those who hold the microphones shout down their opponents through political maneuvering or social ridicule, I'm suspicious. I don't like bullies, especially religious ones.

This means that whenever the anxiety dials up, whenever I sense the adrenaline starting to bubble, I like to whistle in the opposite direction. I don't trust what starts to happen whenever the herd bolts.

I once heard a novelist, late in years, describe the peace he had made with his own writing voice. "In fiction," he wrote, "I think we should have no agenda except to try to be truthful. The shouters-in-thunder can roar from their podiums and pulpits, and I squeak from my corner. They speak to the deaf, but it takes good ears to hear me."

While my letters and sermons may be so bloated as to suggest I have something to say about every issue, the plain fact is I don't. I'm your pastor; I'm not Jesus. Most mornings, I step into the day at least slightly bewildered. I don't know exactly what I believe about some questions. I'm trying to figure things out, just like you are. I trust God gives us wisdom, but sometimes this wisdom comes as a slow drip, not a sudden knowing. Sometimes we only get one meager taste at a time, and we have to sit and wait for more.

I'm learning to be more comfortable in the waiting. I'm not there yet—sometimes I still thrash after answers, when I'm overcome by fear or when my unsettled heart lurches toward anything that seems like safe ground. But I'm getting there. And that prompts a question for all of us: Are we willing to be together, to stay together and love one another, even when we don't know what to say—or when whatever one of us *does* say lands at odds with our own judgments? Can we accept that our greatest gift to one another is how we keep showing up?

Years ago, I called my pastor during a season when I was particularly troubled by the issue du jour. (He's retired now, living on his family land in Washington state. He's in his eighties, and I love him and miss him.) When I called, he answered the phone and, immediately discerning my fretful energy, asked what was bothering me. I responded by unloading the history and describing our church's inflamed dilemma. My pastor had spent a lifetime in the church, so he expressed no shock or dismay; he knew what I was talking about. I told him how the factions lined up and how distressed I was over interpreting Scripture on this matter. "It once seemed so clear to me," I said, pained. "But I don't know now. I don't have any clarity. I don't know what my position should be here."

"Well," my pastor answered, his raspy voice exuding authority and ease, "my position would be to *not* take a position."

I felt immediate relief, then a flood of internal questions. "Can I just punt? Isn't that abdication?"

"I'd call it honesty, Jonas." He paused. "If you don't know, then you *don't know*. To say otherwise would be lying—and I don't think pastors are supposed to do that."

Later, he wrote me a follow-up letter. "It's okay to be confused," he said, "even if for a very long time." He told me about a spiritual director he knew who always insisted that our places of uncertainty are our "necessary path of disorientation."

"I didn't appreciate this at all," he wrote. "However, I think most of us must, at some point or another, lose our bearings. The brand of certitude we like to brandish really has very little to do with God. I wanted to tell you you're in good company. Keep moving and watching. And when the knowledge comes in this matter, if it comes, you'll know. You will sense the freedom and the conviction. Until then, just walk this necessary path."

Our Words & Beverages group just finished Marilynne Robinson's *Home*. One of her main characters, John Ames, a Congregationalist minister in Iowa, may be my favorite fictional clergy—and it's because of moments like this: After enduring yet another roundabout with his best friend, the aging yet still feisty Presbyterian Robert Boughton, Ames says,

I'm not going to apologize for the fact that there are things I don't understand. I'd be a fool if I thought there weren't. And I'm not going to make nonsense of a mystery, just because that's what people always do when they try to talk about it. Always. And then they think the mystery itself is nonsense. Conversation of this kind is a good deal worse than useless. In my opinion.

There's a time for clear-eyed conviction, but it's disingenuous to play this card too often. Too often our "certain convictions" reveal our fear or insecurity or our compulsion to prove we're right. When we do have something genuine to offer, some true word, we must speak. But I believe these words, these moments, will be fewer than we expect.

Don once told me one of the things he found so surprising and restful about our community is how easy we are with one another. "You guys don't seem to be in too much of a hurry, and you like to give folks space to be their own person and process things at their own pace. I appreciate that." I asked Don to explain a little more. "Most of the churches I've known," he continued, "move from one crisis or fight to the next. I didn't see how anyone could live like that." Of course, there are lots of good churches with lots of good people doing lots of good things. And the truth is, sometimes the world *is* in crisis, and sometimes the only right thing to do *is* to roll up our sleeves and join the struggle. But not *all* the time. The tricky part is to know when to step into the fray and when to let the stampede pass us by.

As for me, sometimes I don't speak to a question (even if it's important and even if I have an opinion) simply because it's not my fight. There's no fire in my belly. I'm responsible for some things, but (thank God) I'm not responsible for everything. I am—honestly—unable to be outraged at everything worthy of outrage. I expend my energy in my little corner and trust that God has people in all the other corners of this world to take care of the rest.

We must pay attention to those things that spark the flame, those things that energize us or infuse delight. If there is no call to joy, then I question whether it is my call, my work. I need the laughter as well as the siren. Emma Goldman used to say, "If I can't dance, I don't want to be part of your revolution." I like Luther's angle even better: "If I can't boogey, then you're not playing my kind of blues." Everybody's got their own boogey, and everybody's got their own blues.

Love big. Be well.
Jonas

CONVICTION

Ordinary Time (Pentecost) / June 2010

Dear Friends,

I know these letters are coming in rapid succession. I started with a thought, and I'm compelled to finish it. I promise this pace won't continue. Neither you nor I could endure it.

First, I understand I annoyed a few of you by quoting Emma Goldman. Yes, Emma was indeed an anarchist and atheist. It may be even worse than you've heard. Goldman once wrote an essay called "The Failure of Christianity," and her intent was not merely to denigrate flawed religious institutions in favor of some broad, generic spiritual enlightenment (an idea in vogue even now, though the sentiment's nonsensical to me). No, Emma didn't like God. At all. Nor did she have much good to say about Jesus. Or Buddha. Or Confucius. In 1898, Ms. Goldman thundered from a Detroit pulpit: "I do not believe in God, because

I believe in man. Whatever his mistakes, man has for thousands of years been working to undo the botched job your God has made." Imagine the slack jaws of those filling the pews. Do you think any of them bolted for the door, watching the skies for lightning?

Anyway, whenever I quote someone, it's no rubber stamp for everything else they say or believe. (I couldn't quote myself if *that* were the standard.) The reality is that truth often comes in strange guise. Every person, even under protest, radiates God's image in this world. And we need to hear from a few of God's creatures who don't share our commitments. Besides, I appreciate anyone who can turn a good phrase. Whenever I happen upon a penetrating truth, I think my job is to simply say *Thank you*.

What I've said in a couple of recent letters is clearly incomplete. I *do* believe we encounter much mystery in this world, and we've often done a poor job of honoring it. We could do a better job of keeping silent, watchful, in the face of confusing Scriptures and perplexing times. We must also grapple with our ignorance, our blind spots, our hubris, and our histories (which, unfortunately, include abuses of power and theological debacles). We're human, and we're appropriately skittish about all we don't know. We're sometimes uncertain because we're aware of how we may be wildly mistaken, uninformed, or misinformed. Remember how in a different age Christians insisted, with biblical authority, that the earth was flat? Now we can feel paralyzed by uncertainties, making it difficult for thoughtful people to stand with conviction. How can we know we're not simply clinging to rusty ideas and deluded religious interpretations?

We can't, of course. We can't *know*. At least not if we equate *knowing* with unassailable existential confidence that we've arrived at final truth. This not-knowing taps into one of our greatest fears. More than anything else, some of us are afraid of playing the fool. We fear we'll be shown to be ignorant, unsophisticated, religious Neanderthals. Some of us have been duped by religious teachers or systems, and others of us have suffocated under an oppressive religious subculture. As a consequence, we feel foolish—and angry. And we never, ever intend to be duped again. Many of us wield sarcasm and defensiveness as our weapons. We question everything. We live by always reacting, always trying to prove what we're *not* rather than bravely stepping into the truth of who we *are*, or who we hope to be. We are afraid.

Several weeks ago I had a conversation with Abel Braxton after our Words & Beverages meeting. Our group discussion had been stimulating, but I wanted to talk to Abel about one of his own novels, *Dirt and Thunder*. Hopefully you know Abel won the Anisfield-Wolf Book Award with this wonderful story. Abel's protagonist, Bodie, an aging oil foreman, loses his job to a corporate buyout and has to cobble together a living installing water sprinklers. He lives in a Texas border town, and through the unlikeliest events (I won't ruin the story) becomes friends with a *Coyotaje*, a Mexican people-smuggler. *Dirt and Thunder* is (in my opinion, though Abel cautions me here) as much as anything else a story about a friendship, the bond between two men from two sides of the river. This friendship reminded me of my own hunger for companions; it left me misty more than a few times. I loved the book so much that I only allowed myself a chapter a night for the last three chapters. I just didn't want the story to end.

Bodie welcomes the complexities inherent in his friend's life, how Carlos helps desperate people do desperate things. He doesn't approve of Carlos's smuggling, but he despises even more the fear and prejudice that made it necessary. Bodie himself is a complicated man. He smokes vast amounts of weed, but he's also an old-school cowboy. He stands and removes his hat when a woman enters the room, shooting any man a stern glance if he doesn't do the same. He makes it clear he distrusts politicians and believes our country to be, in general, breeding "weak-minded children ruled by fat-cat miscreants." Bodie is really something—you'll have to read the book and meet him for yourself.

"How did you write Bodie?" I asked Abel. "He felt very true to me, very solid."

Abel thought for a minute before answering. "I'm not exactly sure, though I think you're right. I felt that too. I just discovered Bodie one day, like he'd been sitting there drinking his bottle of Shiner Bock, waiting for me."

Abel told me he believed that Bodie evidenced his growth as a writer, his movement toward writing solid people and solid ideas. "When I first started writing, I felt everything had to be torn apart, every plot dismantled, every character cut low, making sure the flaws were unmistakable, every motivation revealed as suspect. I could have no heroes. My big fear was that someone might accuse me of cliché." Abel rolled his eyes. "Of course, I didn't realize I was writing one massive cliché. Finally I got so bored with myself I went back to work and started over. I ended up writing a character who meant something to me, who *really* meant something to me. I wrote a character with the courage to see something clearly and then live it, and to hell with everything else."

Abel's words put a finger on something I haven't been able to name before, but something that has needled me for a while now. You've heard me say how much I like Rainer Maria Rilke and his advice

69

instructing the young poet to "live the questions."
I truly appreciate Rilke's wisdom. But I'm willing
to bet he didn't mean for us to grapple with every
single question that comes along. And to question
ad nauseam.

I'm all for curiosity and a chastened ego—God
knows we need humility. But it's possible that
something else is happening. We may be surren-
dering to the temptation to go AWOL on our life,
abandoning our responsibility to be somebody
solid in this world. So, yes, let's press into the
questions, but let's make sure they're worthy questions—and let's make sure our questions don't just
provide cover for our fears, an excuse to keep us
from ever having to plant our feet firmly and say,
"This I believe. . . ."

Love big. Be well.
Jonas

BLESSING

Ordinary Time (Pentecost) / October 2010

Dear Friends,

Last Sunday, you may have noticed how the pause before the closing blessing stretched even longer than usual. I always take a few moments, with my hands raised toward you. I go as slow as I think you can handle, looking out over all of you. I love how Don Brady waits with his head high, locks eyes when I turn in his direction, and gives me a big wink. The first few times he did this, I got flustered. Now I search for him, and I wink back. I move slowly because these benedictions are too sacred a thing to rush. Passing a blessing may be the pastor's truest work. I'm charged with the responsibility of reminding you that God loves you and welcomes you, that you are not alone.

Last week, I choked up and had to gather myself. It's not unusual for me to get misty, but this time it took me longer than usual to recover.

I needed more time partly because of the emotion I felt when my eyes landed on Don, after we'd all received news of how his cancer had returned. But it wasn't just about him. I saw all of your faces, and I saw the faces of those who weren't with us on Sunday—as well as the faces of those who aren't with us at all anymore.

Right now, some of you carry such grief. I know the pain some of you experience in your marriages, the despair. I know the sadness and the uncertainty you feel over your children and over their future. Some of us are barely holding our heads above water, while others of us are doing everything we can to hold up someone who's slipping away. For many, the economic hardships have pushed us into terrain we never expected. We have no margin, no security. Many of us feel shame. And many of us are lonely. Some of us are lonely because we ache for a relationship, but others are lonely because the relationship we have has grown cold and brittle— and we feel trapped. Some of us hide who we truly are, afraid that we'll be shunned or that someone will try to "fix" us (or worse, *instruct* us). Some of us wake to fear each morning, and we never escape its talons; fear prods us even through the night.

On Sunday, when I looked out over all of you, my heart strained with the burden of telling you how much God loves you. *Burden* may seem strange here, but this is the word I mean. To pass a blessing is no light thing for me; it's far more than a tidy way to conclude a worship service. These blessings are the words I must say, even if I say nothing else at all. This past Sunday I felt all of this so strongly, and I just needed a little more time before I could speak the words. A little more time to pray that maybe you'd hear them and believe them. And that I would hear them and believe them too.

When I pass a blessing, it's the thing I'm able to do with the firmest conviction. You know me and my fitful faith—but even when I struggle to muster a persuasive sermon from the text, I can still stand before you, stretch my arms wide, and utter the words of Moses: *The Lord bless you and keep you. The Lord make his face to shine upon you and be gracious to you. The Lord turn his face toward you and give you peace.* I can say these words, and I can say them loud and slow. I can linger with you, in those few seconds of quiet, and hope that the good news seeps into us all: *Your Father's face shines on you. Love surrounds you.*

When we're together, passing blessings is crucial. Blessings are both instructive and revelatory. These moments illuminate what it is that all of us are doing every day of our lives. Blessings are not things that happen only in the church building. In fact, most blessings never make it near a pulpit or a stained-glass window. Whenever Sylvie brushes paint onto canvas, she blesses the good world she sees and loves, and she blesses all those who will encounter this beauty she's unveiled. Whenever Abel writes a story that makes us laugh or wonder or hope for something more, it speaks a blessing over this weary world, over every reader. Whenever Don gives one of his bear hugs, that poor soul trying to catch her breath has just received a blessing. Whenever Amy releases one of her infamous expletives over some injustice, or whenever she insists we're all straining too hard and recommends (and I've yet to determine whether she's serious or joking) that we should cancel church every July and August, her needling has just spoken a blessing of rest and comfort. Whenever Dale Benton lays the foundation for a house or Linda Dillman ignites those young minds with multiplication tables, whenever Dalton fits pipe or Hank drops seed in the soil and then frets over it for the dry months to follow, whenever all you mothers and fathers put your plans on hold so you can tend to those mundane and laborious details of home and children—with each of these quotidian acts (and a thousand more), each of you offers a holy blessing.

This is what we are if nothing else: we are people who bless. When I was in college, I rolled my eyes at the older members of my dad's church because they could hardly speak a full sentence without tacking on sentimental goo. Miss Alma was the biggest serial offender: *Well, bless you. Now isn't that a blessing?* I thought that was just syrupy, clichéd. But maybe those folks were passing along the one thing most precious to them, the one thing they had to give away. A few weeks ago, I saw Blake Felton, Stan's son. Blake has tattoos covering his entire right arm and has begun work on his left. Blake rolled up his shirt and showed me the centerpiece: *Blessed* inked in thick, black medieval letters. I imagined Miss Alma's eyes growing wide, confused, then her smile. "Well, that's right, honey. Bless you."

What I want to insist on is this: our entire lives (even when all evidence runs to the contrary) stand shot through with blessing. It's everywhere, and it's our job to speak it, to point it out, to put an arm around friends who can't see it right now and believe it on their behalf. With confidence we say, "Whatever else may be true and despite every competing voice—you belong to God." To insist on blessing in a world where we know such misery, such disruption and inequality and sadness, is not to plead ignorance or brush aside grief and injustice. We do not paint a smiley face on the funeral casket. No, to insist on blessing means we refuse to believe that anything or anyone is ruined. When we insist on blessing, we pronounce our belief that the God who called us *good*, who called the whole world *good*, will not remove the hand of kindness.

But let's have no easy Sunday school misconceptions. To be blessed by God can be a terrifying thing. Saul of Tarsus encountered the Living God and fell to his knees, blind. Prophets trembled when God came calling. Israel hid her face from the thunder, the light, the crushing noise. Who, being honest, has confidence they can withstand God's blessing? I'm not always sure I *want* God.

I'd like to leave you with one of my favorite (and most disturbing) blessings. It's often attributed to St. Francis, but it was actually penned by Sister Ruth Fox, a Benedictine nun from North Dakota:

> *May God bless you with discomfort at easy an-*
> *swers, half-truths, and superficial relationships,*
> *so that you may live deep within your heart.*
> *May God bless you with anger at injustice, op-*
> *pression, and exploitation of people, so that you*
> *may work for justice, freedom, and peace. May*
> *God bless you with tears to shed for those who*
> *suffer from pain, rejection, starvation, and war,*
> *so that you may reach out your hand to comfort*
> *them and to turn their pain into joy. And may*
> *God bless you with enough foolishness to believe*
> *that you can make a difference in this world,*
> *so that you can do what others claim cannot be*
> *done.*

God blessing us with foolishness. I like that.

Love big. Be well.
Jonas

FULL MOON

Ordinary Time (Epiphany) / January 2011

Dear Friends,

Benjamin, my mother's brother, was an old soul, the sort of man who watched the world around him with both delight and befuddlement. Despite his husky frame, Ben carried himself with ease and tenderness, a grizzly who moved among the mountains like a shadow. Ben lived with our family for several years, and I adored him. He became my friend and teacher. In the winter, with his faded flannel shirts, his muscular shoulders, and his salt-and-pepper beard untamed and bushy, Ben looked the part, working with the logging crew harvesting federal land in the valley. He moonlighted as a donkey puncher, the operator of the diesel engine powering the loaders and yarders. But he actually paid the bills working as a research specialist for the city library. With a double major in English and philosophy from the University of North Carolina, he found as much pleasure among the books as he did among the trees and the rivers. "They're both wild country," he told me.

Ben loved to bring his wild, disparate worlds together. He would carry a copy of Dostoevsky, Hemingway, Zane Grey, Mary Anne Evans (he refused to use her pen name, George Eliot, since it was "forced upon her by a gaggle of squawking imbeciles"), or one of his rough-worn copies of Herbert's verse deep into the forest for what he called "a day or two of sanity." In the summertime, he would often invite me along. We spent leisurely hours drinking fireside coffee and talking about the ways of rivers and the ways of women and men and the ways of God—all themes that converged, without contradiction, when I sat with Ben in those primitive spaces. He didn't hesitate to raise questions with me that I couldn't answer—questions that he couldn't answer, either. He entrusted me with the weight of these conversations, these beautiful and frightful mysteries.

Looking back, I believe those experiences invited me to take on one crucial aspect of manhood: the willingness to bear both the light and the dark, the conviction and the quandary, the hopes for our future as well as the clamoring fear that they will never come true. One summer night, one of the last nights we shared under those brilliant stars, Ben built the fire while I gathered water from the stream. Sausages sizzled in the skillet, and coffee gurgled in the pot atop the flames. We poured large cups, steam rising like ghosts. We drank and ate and then sat, not speaking. We watched the flames and the woods and the scattered lights dotting the vastness above us. The only sound was the wind washing through the trees, broken once or twice by coyotes howling up the canyon. Ben picked up a piece of white birch from the ground, carving into the supple wood with his Böker knife.

He was the one who broke the stillness. "Can you imagine what it would have been like, a hundred years ago, to walk into this harsh country, to be on your own, to have all this new possibility but also so much danger?"

Ben peeled and cut, carving what appeared to be the crude head of a bird or perhaps a lopsided apple. For all his admirable qualities, his sculpting skills were underdeveloped. "I once read a novel set in a rugged place like this," he continued. He kept whittling, peeling away thin shavings that scattered on the ground like a light snow. "A boy went missing in the winter, and they didn't find him until spring. Apparently he fell through the river ice. They found him floating under frozen glass, staring up at them like he was wondering what had taken them so dang long." Ben chuckled. "I remember the creepy tales."

"You certainly do," I answered.

"That homesteader lost his wife, lost his son. A wildfire ruined most of his stock and his cabin. I always wondered if he thought it was worth it. The story never said." Ben trimmed curls from his wooden creature. "We don't know what will finally come of us, do we?"

I don't want to leave the wrong impression. Days with Ben were far from somber. At least once a month, he bought me comics, introducing me to his favorites: *Batman*, *Daredevil,* and *Sgt. Fury and His Howling Commandos*. Once, during a heat wave, he woke me before sunup. "Rise and shine. Coffee's in the truck." He drove us to the city pool, where chains wrapped around the gate and *No Trespassing* signs were posted in bright red. Undeterred, Ben climbed the fence. I wavered, uncertain, while he stood on the other side, grinning mischievously. Then he dropped his clothes, his polar-white skin bare as the day he was born. He dove into the water, popped up, and said, "Well, I'm committed— don't leave me stranded." I glanced in every direction, scaled the fence, shucked off my clothes, and jumped into the cool deep. We swam a few laps, then treaded water while we talked and watched the moon tuck into the horizon. "You think *that's* a full moon?" Ben asked. Then he dove underwater and turned three slow flips, his pale keister peeking out with each revolution. I laughed so hard I had to grab the side of the pool to stay afloat.

I don't know why I remember that morning so clearly, or why exactly I'm telling you this story now. This kind of foolishness wasn't new to me. I was, after all, an adolescent boy with raging hormones and regular lapses in judgment. But there I shared a guileless foolishness with a man I respected, a man of wisdom and knowledge. I couldn't name it then, but I think that day infused in me the truth that while there's a kind of foolishness we ought to shed as we mature, a naiveté or a crassness that does us harm, there's also a foolishness we must cling to—a refusal of the charlatan seriousness that steals our playfulness, dulls our curiosity, and chokes out our holy rebellion against the grim and narrow life. There's a certain childlike foolishness that's essential to those of us who crave joy. But we haven't learned how to distinguish these very different types of foolishness, and I fear we've lost much amid the confusion.

I hope we'll help one another be appropriately foolish. I hope we'll be a community living full-throttle toward joy. Life is too short to waste time on the alternatives.

Two weeks ago, I went with Don to one of his chemo treatments. He told me his hair had been falling out in clumps much faster than it had during his first bout, so he'd gone to the barbershop and told them to shave him clean. "I'm slick and shiny now," he said. I wondered if he would feel self-conscious, but I needn't have worried about that. When I picked him up for his treatment, he wore a black t-shirt printed with these words in white letters: *It's not a bald spot. It's a solar panel for a love machine.*

All the nurses doted on Don; they'd already grown to love him like we do. I told him I wished he'd known Ben—they would have been fast friends. Don knows something about the kind of life I'm trying to live, the kind of life I hope we all experience.

Love big. Be well.
Jonas

THE WORLD WHOLE

Holy Week / April 2011

Dear Friends,

I've continued to think a lot about Ben since I wrote last. I've thought more about his influence and how it forms me as a Christian and a pastor. Holy Week always draws my mind to death's sorrows and to all those I love who have already pierced death's veil.

Ben saw the world whole, whereas for much of my life I saw it mostly as a collection of sundry parts. He drank in the fragrance of aspens and Scripture and honeysuckle. He allowed himself to be moved by good rye whiskey, a beautiful woman, or a great sentence. I might find him elbow-deep in grease, oil, and carburetor parts, or I might watch him grapple with sorrows or chew on a knotty idea for weeks. Ben believed that to dare, to fail, to pray—that these were essential lines in our life's story. When I was in seminary, I once asked him how he stayed a man of faith with all he knew and all he had experienced—all that many assumed to be contradictory. "Well," he answered, "I've found I just need to keep getting a bigger set of eyes." I'm not even sure exactly what that means. I just remember how Ben had a mind and a heart large enough to hold everything at once, how with him there was enough room for so many things to live side by side. He had a generous view of life.

If the idea of providence means anything, then it must at least mean that our life consists of all manner of truths and experiences we would never imagine and could never orchestrate. The old mystics liked to say that "all is gift." I still scratch my head over this idea, but I'm learning to trust that everything we encounter, every beauty and every tragedy, invites us deeper into God, deeper into our truest selves.

In other words, to become more like God (more *Christian*, if it helps to say it that way) is in fact to become more human. Jesus showed us what it looks like to be God, but Jesus also showed us what it looks like to be truly human. We often fear our human bodies, our human urges and aspirations, our human frailties. But to be Christian is to become more and more human.

More human, more joyful, more curious, more hopeful, more aware—I want more of this life we call *sacred*. More of the family given to us, the histories before us, the land around us, the desire and pleasures (and despairs) within us.

My family and I hadn't been here long when Luther asked me why we chose to move to Granby. "Because it seemed like most of you wanted me," I told him, "and I found myself wanting you too." Our arrival had nothing to do (on my end) with moving up the ecclesial ladder, and nothing to do (on your end) with any quixotic notions of securing a pastoral savior. I should probably only speak for myself, but I think maybe we just like one another. Could that be enough?

I know I feel hope again—and I can tell you, this is no small thing. I have hope that perhaps we've found one another at the right time. Perhaps, like Esther, we are here "for such a time as this. . . ." I wonder if we might learn, together, more of what it means to live in this one single place, to love the years we've been given, to cherish our responsibilities to one another and to our land and our community. Taking our cue from Jesus, we can learn to be truly human and to love this good world, as we work toward our shared redemption.

Naturalist, farmer, and unintentional theologian Wendell Berry wrote, "Farming by the measure of nature, which is to say the nature of the particular place, means farmers must tend farms they know and love, farms small enough to know and love, using tools and methods they know and love, in the company of neighbors they know and love." This is true for farmers, true for friends, true for pastors—true for all of us.

The first time I met Miss Nelson, at the pot-luck after church on the Sunday my family visited Granby, she caught my eye and waved me over. She pushed her walker away and patted the folding chair next to her. "Sit down, Reverend, sit down." I obeyed. She asked about the seminary I had attended (thankfully, she approved) and queried for a few more details about our previous church and the years I'd been away from the pulpit. She asked me about the books I was reading, but then she crossed her arms on the table, looked me in the eye, and said, "So, Reverend, who are your people?" It was obvious that all the interview up till then had just been the warm-up. Who were the people who had brought me into this world? What was our history? What did we love? What were we committed to?

I filled Miss Nelson in as best I knew how. When I finished telling my family story, she grabbed my hand and squeezed it. "Well, Reverend, I've heard what I need to know. Everybody ought to be able to explain about their people."

Thinking about Ben and Miss Nelson, I'm discovering more about why I want to write these sporadic letters. I appreciate both the freedom and the slowness we enjoy through them. I write them when I can, and you read them (or not) with the same leisure. I want to keep scratching around these questions I raise, to help us remember (to help *me* remember) that this human life in this physical place is the life God has given us. I want to learn more about what it means to live together well, as God's people.

Whatever else we've been told, I'm convinced these things are at the heart of being the church. This life (not some other) is the way of our redemption. As Teresa of Ávila reminded us, "The whole way to heaven is heaven itself."

> Love big. Be well.
> *Jonas*

THE RUSE OF AUTHENTICITY

Ordinary Time (Pentecost) / June 2011

Dear Friends,

We have entered our second (and longest) stretch of Ordinary Time for the year, where we rehearse again the stories of Jesus's life and Israel's sojourn while we slog through a long, mundane stretch of very plain days. We've completely spent all the enlivening anticipation Advent evokes. We've shot through the many delights Christmastide offers. We've persevered (thank God) through Lent's intense diligence. We've expended Easter's raucous joy and Pentecost's invigorating flurry. And here we are now, again, plodding forward, trying to help one another make it through. One foot in front of the other, one prayer after another.

Christian faith is not primarily an ethereal religion but a grit-and-grind, in-this-world undertaking. And in this world, few things hold us in their oppressive grip more than our checkbook and our calendar. This must be why God gave us practical ways to rebel against these despotic powers. God tells us to give our dollars away; God also tells us to stop our work and rest. I'm glad God instructed me to be generous with my money, to regularly let loose of more than I think prudent. I can be a bit tight-fisted, so I need help prying open my wallet. Left to myself, I'd also fritter my weeks away. I'd never rest with purpose. I'm glad God said, *Hey, every six days or so, put your tools down. Relax. Blow off some steam. I mean it.*

For many of us, however, the church year is about as familiar as the Periodic Table of Elements. We've heard of a few of the names on the chart, but on the whole, the diagram's a mystery. We may or may not utilize these gifts of tithe and Sabbath, but most of us at least know about them. Likewise, we enjoy our Christmas Eve candlelight service and our Easter festivities. But beyond that, we're mostly in the dark when it comes to talking about the Christian calendar.

That's why I want to think a bit more about one of the gifts of the church year that we often overlook: how it gives us a way to practice our faith even when we do not *feel* our faith. We are not asked, come February or March, whether or not we'd like to repent and make room for God. Lent simply instructs us to get to it. No one asks us whether or not we feel up to celebrating Easter.

We're not asked to peer deep inside to see if our souls feel like throwing a drain-the-bank party. No, Easter simply hands us a fifty-day feast and says, *Go do joy*.

Yes, our feelings are important, essential, but we give them too much say. For many of us, our feelings have gotten a little big for their britches.

I have confessed to you—perhaps more than you'd like—how there are countless questions that regularly trip me up, and there are Sundays when the last thing I feel like doing is standing up to give a sermon. (*Aha*, you say, *so that's the problem*.) But thankfully, it's not my job to feel the passion of the sermon. I've been given a charge, and when I put on that stole and open that Book, I'm speaking not only for myself but also for all those who've come before me, alongside all those who make up this mystery we know as church. I've been handed a creed and a text and told to do the best I'm able.

Some days, my feelings are simply going to have to figure out how to keep up. Odd, isn't it? There are days, too, when I don't feel the electricity of love for Alli (or she for me), but I announce my love to her, *live* my love toward her, nonetheless. And I'm not being inauthentic in this. I'm demonstrating how my love runs far deeper than my whims or confusions. I promised fidelity, and this pledge to faithfulness provides the sturdy ground of truth.

The same can be said for faith. How we *feel* in

a given season (or on a given Sunday) is likely not as important as we think. So we can free ourselves from our obsessive introspection over how we feel. And let's face it: the whole idea that we can arrive at some pure expression of faith—or even some pure understanding of God—is as ridiculous as it is oppressive. As Karl Barth said, "Let us set aside our investigation of God. God searches us. Our mind is never right." Attentiveness to our emotions may tell us where our heart is, but it cannot be trusted to tell us where *God* is. Only God can do that. And God promises to be with us whether or not we feel it—or understand it.

When I started writing these letters, I said I wanted to help us remember how to live good lives together, in this one place we've been given and in this precise moment in time. I wanted to encourage us to be present to our life and to each other. I wanted us to be true, to be authentic and faithful. That was the truth, and still is. But I *don't* want to give any energy to this ruse of authenticity, to this stifling brand of introspection. I want you to see me and hear my story, and give me room to be myself. And I want to do the same for you. I hope we'll call each other out of the shadows, that we'll invite one another toward joy.

So I invite us all to give money even when we don't feel generous. I encourage us all to take a break even when we're convinced everything will fall apart if we take our foot off the pedal. I invite us all to live in the story of the Christian year even when we don't feel inspired, to pray with each other and break bread with each other even when our faith seems to have petered out. It's okay if you're not sure about things; I'm not sure about things at least half the time, either.

Hank Pierce and I were talking about these ideas not too long ago, and he said, "So you're telling me to fake it 'til I make it?" Not exactly. But close.

Let's shake off the fear and the hesitation and just *do* what we believe until our mind or our imagination or our desires catch up.

Love big. Be well.
Jonas

WHISKEY AND BISCUITS

Advent / November 2011

Dear Friends,

Last week's edition of *The New Yorker* included a short story introducing Randall Finch, the elderly proprietor of a Cincinnati bookshop. A few years earlier, Finch surrendered to Amazon and abandoned selling new titles. This actually suited him well, as he preferred books that passed hands before they arrived on his shelves. "I like my books the way I like my women," he said: "well-traveled and with subtle creases." The fuller truth was that Finch was a contrarian and had a general beef with literary fashion. The last time he read a book appearing on the current *Times* bestseller list was 1971: Walker Percy's *Love in the Ruins*. He made this exception partly because the title coincided with his still-fresh experience of a broken heart, but mainly because he always, always supported Percy. Finch's home, his heritage back at least six

93

generations, was New Orleans; and he stayed true. He named his first daughter Nola, named his shop *Books & Jazz,* and read Percy whether or not it conflicted with his standing protest.

My point is that this Finch piece was a good story. One of Randall Finch's eccentricities was his obsession with beets. He ate a beet-and-bacon sandwich, on rye, at 11:30 every weekday of his life. He locked the front door of his shop, pulled out the *Cincinnati Herald,* opened his thermos of English breakfast tea, and read local news and obituaries until his stomach was full and his fingers black and purple.

Finch's fixation stayed with me because it reminded me of my grandmother, Gigi McAnn, and a fateful afternoon when I must have been six or seven. Gigi also loved beets, and though she knew I held my nose at just the sight of those red monstrosities, she cornered me with her beet salad one day. "Now, Jonas, honey, you've never had it this way. It's so sweet, it tastes like jam." I wasn't convinced, but after much cajoling, I complied. Immediately, my stomach revolted. I clenched my teeth together, trying not to gag, and looked at Gigi, wide-eyed. She pulled me to the kitchen counter, where I spewed maroon chunks into her bleach-white sink. Then she turned on the faucet and patted my back. "Well, Jonas, it's settled then. You don't like beets."

Gigi has been gone for two decades, but who she was and what she instilled in her family remain. She taught us about gardening: to pull weeds and water dry soil and keep an eye out for beetles and groundhogs. And she told us stories. Among the tomatoes, the beans, and the corn, she told us about her father, who emigrated from Canada and started a hardware business, and her mother, who managed their local newspaper in 1917, when two of the male editorial staff members received draft notices for what became World War I. Most of what I know about our family history came from Gigi.

The memory of her that's most precious to me is our celebration of my eighteenth birthday. Whenever a grandchild turned eighteen, Gigi would invite us over for a few hours. So it was no surprise for me to receive her call. "Jonas—Happy Birthday, honey. Could you come over this afternoon?" Gigi and I sat on her front porch, and she handed me a gift-wrapped box from Rose's Department Store. Inside was a rust-brown corduroy jacket with leather elbow patches, just as I'd wanted. Some grandparents gifted packs of Fruit of the Looms or a lunch trip to Luby's. But Gigi knew us. She watched and listened and didn't forget.

"I have one more thing for you," Gigi told me. After we followed the scent of buttermilk and flour into the kitchen, she opened the oven and pulled out hot biscuits, golden and lopsided, bursting from the pan. She placed three on a plate in front of me, then reached into the back of a side drawer and pulled out two shot glasses. Next, after climbing atop a stepstool, she recovered a bottle of Woodford Reserve Bourbon from the far corner of the top shelf. As I watched, goggle-eyed, she poured a tall shot into each glass and finally sat down beside me.

"Jonas," she asked, "have you ever drunk before?"

If Gigi had appeared in bloomers while levitating down the hallway, the shock would have been no greater. "Well . . . you know . . . a little . . . not much, just once . . . maybe twice. . . . I didn't like it."

"It's stout, to be sure."

I waited for her to continue. She held her glass in her hand, her mind remembering something or praying for someone or working something out. At last she spoke. "Jonas, when my brothers turned eighteen, my dad, though he was a teetotaler every other day of his life, served each of them a shot of whiskey, as apparently his father had done with him." Gigi went quiet again, rubbing her glass with her thumb. "Though we had to hide it from Mother, my dad did the same for me, and I have never forgotten it."

She raised her glass to her lips and nodded for me to do the same. I took a sip, then hacked and winced and pounded my fist on my chest. Someone had lit a match and tossed it down my throat.

Gigi placed her glass back on the table. "It's something to sit here with you, two more of us in this long line. Years from now, I want you to remember that you drank Woodford's at this table with me."

I coughed a few more times and wiped my eyes. I felt like I was spinning on a Tilt-A-Whirl, jolted by the liquor and grasping after what was happening—Gigi and me and this bottle of flaming liquid.

She cupped her shot glass. "And one more thing. . . ." She pointed her bony finger at my nose. "You grabbed that glass way too easy. Don't you ever let me catch you with a bottle. If I do, I'll tear into your backside."

Before I left, we ate a dozen biscuits between us. I would never look at Gigi or a bottle of Woodford the same way again.

It strikes me, as I'm writing this, that my Grandma McAnn was a liturgist. She fashioned a life and a rhythm that formed in me a way of seeing the world and a way of seeing my place in the world. Some of us weary of the church's liturgy and wonder if it isn't time to chuck these weathered forms. But I couldn't possibly agree. How could I ever believe it appropriate to discard, either in my family or in my faith, the very practices that have made me who I am, the very practices I hope have helped make my own children who they will be?

You recall, I'm sure, that *liturgy* means "the work of the people." It is our work to remember God. It is our work to remember who we are. It is our work to remember we're part of a family, a long line of women and men, strangers and strugglers and dreamers who have all gathered around this table Jesus made possible. Even though we are continually immersed in wonder, it is difficult for us to remember how this beauty rests everywhere.

And of course, liturgy is something we do together. None of us contrived these prayers or blessings on our own. My grandmother invited me into her story, and the Church (all the mothers and fathers before us) invites us into her story. The invitation arrives every week. What a relief it is to know we don't carry this faith alone. Liturgy allows us to affirm truths we might not even believe just yet, or truths we're simply too exhausted to hold up with our own weary prayers.

If liturgy bores you from time to time, you're in good company. I can't imagine anyone who's stuck with anything worth sticking with who hasn't had more than a few experiences of feeling half-hearted and carried along by others' prayers. This is precisely one of liturgy's greatest gifts: it invites us to be carried along.

Of course, liturgy isn't just what happens on Sunday. We carry the liturgy with us into our lives. We do this work day after day. We do the work of faith, the work of hope, the work of love. We pull the nine to five so we can put potatoes on the table. We try to speak up against wrongs and reach out to a friend who's hit a rough patch. We show up for our kids, taking them to softball practice and taking out a second mortgage for orthodontics and giving them the very best of ourselves until they load up and launch into life on their own (and even then we love them and worry for them). None of this is glamorous. All of this is our work.

A week or so ago, I began chatting with one of the regulars at Stu's (one of the members of the Order of the Roasted Bean). Our conversation moved to my role as a "professional Christian," as this friend put it. He's half-baffled and half-intrigued by why anyone would spend their life in ministry. I admitted how life in the church (whether or not you're a pastor) can sometimes lead to lethargy, boredom, and frustration. "Well," my friend said, "do you think meeting up with these hooligans at Stu's all these years is always a party? It can be downright tedious. But we keep showing up. It's important to just show up."

Showing up, doing the work, being together— that's our liturgy. And it matters.

Love big. Be well.
Jonas

THE COMMON SOUND

Ordinary Time (Epiphany) / February 2012

Dear Friends,

Since Abel makes his living with words, and since Amy feeds her voracious curiosity, they both possess a far more eclectic reading list than I do. One of them inevitably suggests an author or a genre I would never venture to explore if left to myself. This is one reason why it's good to read alongside people different from you—or go to church alongside people you might not naturally choose. If I only encounter my own opinion or prejudice, I miss out on all kinds of truth and beauty. And without disruptive input from others, I'll stay more dense than I have to be.

Still, when Abel recommended we read Wallace Stegner's *Angle of Repose*, I protested. I told him that, years earlier, I had labored through Stegner's *The Big Rock Candy Mountain,* and I just didn't think I could endure another laborious, plodding novel leading me nowhere.

Undeterred by my reluctance, Abel persisted. "Give it another whirl, Jonas," he told me. "I think Stegner's your kind of man. Don't insist you have to know where he's taking you. Just watch what he's doing."

Darn if Abel wasn't right. I discovered that everything Stegner wrote hums at a low frequency. He sought to come to terms with the one life he knew, to offer his experiences and confusions with unadorned authenticity, even sparseness. "I don't like big noisy scenes," he once admitted, "in fiction or in life. I avoid riots and mass meetings. It would embarrass me to chase fire engines. I have a hard enough time making sense out of what my life hands me without going out and hunting more exciting events." He believed our daily lives are significant just as they are, worthy of great attention and providing perpetual conduits of joy.

With new eyes, I turned to *Angle of Repose,* where Lyman Ward, the wheelchair-bound historian, puts his pen to the project he's neglected for decades: his grandmother's biography. Divorced from his wife and estranged from his son, Ward seeks to reestablish some bond with his kin, even if their lives exist for him only as memories. *Repose*, which won Stegner the Pulitzer, lumbers more than I would like. Still, with genuine gratitude and admiration, I would now simply describe Stegner's writing as *plain*—solid words, born out of deep conviction.

Whether or not we read him, Stegner has something to teach us all. Too often, we want the grand gestures, the high profits, the big people. If we run after these things, I fear we may lose ourselves. We may abandon our actual lives. Stegner believed—as I do—that we cannot afford this kind of wholesale abandonment. It costs us far too much.

Later, recognizing he had me hooked, Abel sent me the link to a Stegner lecture. "Listen to this," he urged. "This, I think, is what it's all about." As I listened, Stegner explained that he wanted his writing to be "part of the common sound." When he said this, I was so struck by the rightness of his words that I had to write them down.

With this single line, Stegner sums up so much of what I hope for myself and for our community. We do not need to be anything other than ourselves, people who bear God's image and God's love. We do not need to impose anything upon our neighbors or upon our own God-given sensibilities. We do not need to live some other life in some other place. We simply need to be part of the common sound. Here. With one another. That will be enough.

Love big. Be well.
Jonas

PRAYING INCOGNITO

Eastertide / May 2012

Dear Friends,

Several weeks ago, Luther and Abel took me fly-fishing. It was awful. The company was splendid, the scenery restorative. Still, my frustration idled at a high RPM the entire time. They were patient teachers, but my cast dribbled and jerked. The arc of my line held no flight or grace; it slapped against the water with all the artistry of a belly flop. I snagged a branch that, for any fisherman beyond the age of four, would have been out of harm's way. After my second time catching the tree, Abel said, "You can go for those if you want, but they're hard to eat." Luther laughed, but I just mumbled an expletive and wrestled with my twisted, tangled line.

Driving home, Luther asked, "You know what I like about fly-fishing?"

"I do not," I answered. Why would anybody torture themselves with this galling pastime?

"I like how you're just in it. You're in the water, in the woods. Everything's happening around you."

I've concluded that my problem (aside from how I have no idea what I'm doing on the river) is my focus on casting properly, on actually *catching fish*. Luther, however, comes to the river in a much different way. "I like being in the water," he explained, "with the breeze and the scent and the solitude. Even when I don't catch anything, I come back different than when I left."

The same week of my fly-fishing calamity, I had another conversation. "I've been trying to pray for a very long time," a friend told me, "but nothing happens, and I'm sick of it."

I have only two or three primary jobs as a pastor, and one of these jobs is to help you learn how to pray. The only problem I've had with this assignment is that I need a tutor myself. If you want to push my spiritual insecurity button, start pressing me on my practice of prayer. Lately, my primary instructor has been Sister Brenda, the nun I meet with at Our Lady of Angels. The last time I asked her for help praying, she asked me, "What do you love to do?" I must have looked confused, because she went at the question again. "When do you feel relaxed and joyful?" I told her I enjoyed walking in the woods and writing. "Do those things," she said, "and listen for God while you're at it."

So when my frustrated friend asked if I had anything to say about prayer, I plagiarized and passed along Sr. Brenda's instructions. In the meantime, I've continued to think about my struggles with fly-fishing and my struggles with prayer alongside each other.

Prayer is not so much about securing our requests or completing a prescribed spiritual practice. It is simply communion with God. When we pray (i.e., when we receive God's love and return our love back to God), what happens with our prayers (whether or not we receive our requests or feel changed in any way) is of secondary importance. We have been with God, and God has been with us. To borrow Luther's words, "Even if we don't catch anything, we come back different than when we left." Mainly, what I'm saying is this: Relax. Prayer is not something we accomplish; it's something we enter. It's pretty darn hard to do prayer wrong.

Still, I don't want to imply that prayer is only concerned with some internal flutter of the heart. I'm not a fan of bumper-sticker sentiments like "Prayer doesn't change God; it changes us." They strike me as seriously off the mark. When Abraham wrangled with God, the situation shifted in Sodom. When Moses raised his arms in petition to God, the Israelites beat back their enemies; but when Moses dropped his arms, their enemies advanced. When biblical characters like Paul and

Hannah prayed, stuff happened. No less a character than Jesus once uttered the confusing line instructing us that if we would only pray in faith, we would receive whatever we asked.

Look, I'll be the first to confess that I don't have the foggiest clue how prayer works—or how seemingly contradictory truths (like how to blend God's providence with our meaningful participation, for starters) play together here. But here's two things I do know and believe: prayer matters, *and* we don't have to get it right. Jesus calls us to prayer, and yet Jesus, with the Spirit, has already prayed for us and makes up for our lack. That seems like the best of both worlds to me.

Another thing: Prayer includes a wider bandwidth than we often think. Prayer means talking to God, but even more, prayer means listening to God, listening *for* God. Prayer is action. Prayer is sitting still. Prayer happens through our hopes and through our tears. Prayer happens through songs and mental images, through smells and sounds and tastes. Prayer happens with words, and (thank goodness) when our words completely fail us. Prayer happens in any place and in any way open to God's presence. When Sylvie told me about the plans she and Abel had to walk the Camino de Santiago, she explained how it would be a pilgrimage filled with prayer and wine. "Two ways of doing the same thing," Sylvie said. Indeed.

Sylvie knows something about prayer. I've learned that for her, to pray is to paint. She'll tell you how over the years, her physical labor—the mixing of the oils and the movement of the brush—has become the only language she can manage. Painting—this grammar of color, shape, and texture—allows her to both mourn troubles and express gratitude. At times spare, at times lavish, her canvases offer her benediction. Sylvie weaves litanies of loss and hope into her parched, desolate prairies. With a brush, she offers her petitions for the world and the people she holds dear. She invokes the love she believes will, in the end, hold all of them together. Seeing Sylvie's paintings, I whisper *Amen*.

"The world is crowded with God," wrote C. S. Lewis. "God walks everywhere incognito. And the incognito is not always hard to penetrate. The real labour is to remember, to attend. In fact, to come awake. Still more, to remain awake." This idea alone could dismantle much of what we've all been taught about prayer.

And the last thing: I believe prayer to be a communal act more than an individual one. I pray best when I'm walking with someone, or when I'm sitting alongside a few of you on a Sunday morning, or when I'm visiting with you in your home—anyplace where conversation turns to our desires and our sorrows. When I pray alone (and if I'm not walking or moving), chances are I barely make it five minutes before my eyes droop. I used to feel ashamed about this. Now I simply view it as further confirmation that for prayer, we really do need one another. This is why we have written prayers for all of us to say each Sunday, and why we use the collect prayers Christians around the world will pray on this same day. We do not pray alone.

This is also why (and I hope I don't lose you here) I find such comfort in praying with the saints. The book of Hebrews tells us we have a cloud of witnesses surrounding us, and if the saints are, even now, alive in Christ, then why would they not pray with us and for us? The people of God extend beyond mortal time; we are joined together forever. As I see it, asking our spiritual foremothers and forefathers to pray for us is no stranger than asking you to pray for me. In the fourth century, St. Jerome talked about the martyrs, finally healed and whole in God, praying for all of us who would follow them. I certainly hope this is true. I'll take all the prayers I can get.

The bottom line is that prayer isn't nearly as complicated or as one-dimensional as we've made it out to be. Prayer offers us a gift: to hear and encounter God amid the tangle and groan and delight of our common experience. It's not some ecstatic spiritual state so much as simply putting one foot in front of the other. As St. Francis insisted, "The result of prayer is life."

Love big. Be well.
Jonas

P.S. I realize I didn't say much of anything practical here. I didn't talk about models for prayer (contemplative prayer, daily hours, lectio, Ignatian practices, etc.). I left this out partly because I'm no expert on any of them, but also because I think that whatever model works for you is the one you should use. Pray as you can, not as you can't. Some of us will need to be freewheeling at times, to experiment a little. Here I should confess, though my inner Merton cringes to admit this, that my schedule for prayer is, shall we say, *elastic*. My main problem with "quiet times" (is this still in our vocabulary?) is that I want my whole life to be quiet.

THE CREEDS

Ordinary Time (Pentecost) / September 2012

Dear Friends,

Recently I've been asked several times why we say the Apostles' Creed and the Nicene Creed on Sundays. It's a good question that deserves a good answer.

First, it's important to remember that we don't just *say* the creeds—we *pray* them. The creeds end with *Amen*. When we pray, we converse with the Holy Trinity, the God of the universe. When we pray these lines from the creeds, we're not only reciting doctrine. We're putting ourselves into the right posture again, returning to the place of healing and wholeness, as creatures before our Maker. In these prayerful creeds, we acknowledge that we are finite and that only God knows the contours of our desperate hearts and our fickle minds. Only God knows our deepest truths.

Second, the creeds do not merely catalog theological facts. They narrate a story, recounting for us God's actions on our behalf. The creeds assure us that God, in Jesus, has created us and rescued us and that the Spirit guides us even now. We are not alone. Not ever.

Third, the creeds (like every kind of prayer) are, by their very nature, communal acts. I side with the Orthodox Christians who say *we believe* rather than *I believe*, but no matter the verbiage, the creeds' very existence affirms the essential truth that faith must be something we discern together and strive to sustain together. When someone tells me they're not sure they can say the creed because they're no longer certain they believe it, I always ask them if they could try, at least for a bit, simply trusting the community of faith. Can we borrow the faith of those who have believed this story and prayed these words and hung their hopes on these truths for nearly two millennia? Yes—and thank God for that. My personal existential crisis every Sunday morning at ten may not be the most reliable, or even noteworthy, barometer. Our individual dilemmas and hesitations are important, but they don't trump everything else.

Some of you have told me you believe that creeds reflect an unenlightened version of religion—or worse, that they function as a power play where the majority silences the minority. Some of us cringe whenever any Christian community insists on any core story, any foundational truths, on which their hope rests. That feels too restrictive and narrow. But even the most progressive communities operate with established expectations (either explicit or implicit) for acceptable behavior and viewpoints. And most every stripe of Christian community has certain core principles they believe to be essential.

Few, for instance, would be willing to abandon the core convictions that Jesus calls us to reject violence and to love the other. We might even say these convictions are non-negotiable parts of the Christian message. All of us have a creed.

It's actually impossible *not* to have a creed. Either we have a creed that is thoughtful and reflective, one we have reached through carefully navigating the interplay of our faith, our community, and our conviction—or we have a creed that is ad hoc, reactive, and no sturdier than our own capricious impulses. As Jaroslav Pelikan liked to say, "The only alternative to tradition is bad tradition."

The question, then, is what creed will we follow? I don't trust myself—or even my moment in history—to give the final word on this matter. I choose to trust the God who raised Jesus from the dead, the God who speaks through the Living Spirit. I choose to trust the community of faith, imperfect as she has been. I choose to trust God's love and providence as God's people have labored across time and history to hear God's story and obey. You, of course, must decide for yourself who you trust and where you will give yourself, where you will say, *I believe*. No one can do this for you.

You know that Don, thank God, has been feeling stronger. He's finally felt good enough to handle his motorcycle again. Last week, he invited me take a ride with him on the Blue Ridge Parkway. I haven't been on a bike in years, but I borrowed a Yamaha and quickly fell back in the groove of that powerful rumble on the open road. At lunchtime, we pulled in for lunch at an outdoor diner. Over greasy burgers and greasier onion rings, I told Don that I used to notice how, when we said the creed, he'd bow his head and stand there, silent—but how lately I'd seen him joining in. "What changed?" I asked.

"Well, I try to be honest—and for a stretch there I was bothered by how I didn't have a handle on some of what we were saying . . . still don't." Don showed no shame with his declaration—he looked like a man who'd just admitted 2 + 2 = 4. "But then I understood you to say that it's not just my own smarts or faith at work here, but that I'm joining the faith of the church. This was a load off my shoulders. And I've been saying the creed ever since."

I don't know if Don noticed, but I fought back tears. I *had* said those words, but I hadn't heard them in my own heart the way Don had taken them into his. I managed a few bites, then turned to Don. "Thank you," I said. And I meant it more than he knew.

Love big. Be well.
Jonas

ADVENT AND CHRISTMASTIDE

Advent / November 2012

Dear Friends,

Now we've stepped into Advent's enchantment. These are some of my favorite days. These are days for waiting and watching, days of quiet expectation. To be clear, Advent is *not* Christmas. Advent (or the Nativity Fast, for our Orthodox friends) prepares us for Christmas, but we have to walk the road—we haven't arrived yet. We live, for the moment, in taut anticipation. We long for what's ahead, for what has not yet come. Advent gives us a language for what so many of the days and seasons of our life are like for us—we live *between*. Between hope and fulfillment, between desire expressed and desire fulfilled. As my friend Robert says, we live between the dreaming and the coming true.

During Advent, the lectionary gives us James's words: *Be patient therefore, beloved, until the coming of the Lord....* Commencing our Christian year anew, Advent provides an important corrective to the fables governing our lives. We expect our starts to bolt from the gate. Energy! Exertion! Strategic master plans! But with Advent we start by waiting. We Sabbath.

Alli tells me that Advent is the best time to plant tulips. She plops those clumpy bulbs in the cold, crusty ground, and then she waits. I forget about them, about the secret flowers unfolding under that dead dirt. But then, one marvelous spring day, life erupts. One afternoon last spring, I came home to find Alli sitting on a blanket, basking among the first buds—white, orange, and violet. "I told you they were coming," she said, radiant. "You just have to wait. And hope." This is the same lesson I could have learned from the apostle James, who tells us that much of our life will be like that of the long-suffering farmer who "waits for the precious crop from the earth, being patient with it...."

Patient *with it*—this is the crucial turn. To be patient doesn't merely mean we're applying the brakes. And living patiently doesn't mean camouflaging our annoyance with ambiguity or delay. True patience means learning how to be *with* our life, to be present and curious and perhaps, above all, tenaciously hopeful.

Advent frustrates those of us who want to move

fast, to get things done. But it may offer sweet relief to those of us who live at the jagged edges, who are accustomed to the crush of disappointment, of fear. Advent comes first for those who have made a wreck of things, for those who carry a legitimate complaint, for those whose existence teeters on the brink. If there is no raw, raspy voice somewhere in the hollows of our soul that every now and again whispers Isaiah's words into the ravaging night—*God, please . . . Please tear open the heavens and come down*—then some of what Advent offers will always escape us.

And to be disconnected from the way of Advent is okay; it simply means we're not yet ready. But we should tuck this letter in our pocket because someday . . . someday we *will be*.

It took me the longest time to understand how the song "Twelve Days of Christmas" really was about Christmas lasting twelve days. You may have noticed we don't sing Christmas hymns until those days draw close. Before that, it's Advent hymns, songs of longing and hopes deferred, songs praying for love to come. Then, after all our ache and loneliness and fears have had their say, we gather in the candlelight of Christmas Eve. We announce hope's arrival. And we proclaim that God has not abandoned us, that God is with us. Then we can let "Joy to the World" rise up to shake the rafters.

Look, I know that pastors are expert at loading

on guilt, but that's not my goal here. I'm not telling you to cancel all your plans during these weeks and force yourselves to practice some kind of minimalist Advent observance. I really don't have a clue about how we're to do this better, given the numerous demands of our lives. I just want to remind you that the ache, the longing, for what we do not yet experience is real. I feel it with you. And I want you to know that the joy is even *more* real. Christmastide isn't here yet, but it's coming. And I hope that when it does arrive, you'll make the space and take the time to truly celebrate it, to revel in the goodness. God knows we need it.

One way we can honor Advent together is by joining in a vigil for all those who've lost friends and family over the past year and all who've experienced significant hardship. For many, the coming holiday season prompts despair, not joy. To remember them, Amy and the Order of the Roasted Bean are organizing a candlelight vigil on the square, across from Stu's, on Thursday, December 20, at eight P.M. And they've asked us to join them. Tom and the good folks at Felton's Garage will be bringing hot mulled cider and apple fritters from the Donut Palace for everyone. Dress warm. I'll meet you there.

Love big. Be well.
Jonas

THE PEOPLE WHO BURY YOU

Ordinary Time (Epiphany) / January 2013

Dear Friends,

Recently I've been reading Jürgen Habermas, a German philosopher who's one of our pre-eminent intellectuals. Habermas came of age during the destruction wrought by the Nazi regime. Ever since, he's tried to make ethical sense of human societies, of how we've become who we are and how we might become something better in the future. I'm told that if one were to trace his intellectual journey (a job I'm not equipped to do), his shift from excoriating religion to endorsing its merits follows a logical progression. But I'm less interested in philosophical connect-the-dots than the story he recounts as a moment of illumination.

Max Frisch, a noted Swiss novelist and a friend of Habermas, was diagnosed with terminal colorectal cancer in 1989. The doctors told Frisch he had two years to live, and he took advantage of the time to plan his own funeral. Though he spurned religious belief, he requested that his memorial be held in St. Peter's Church, the oldest parish in Zürich. But he didn't want a priest to preside, and he explicitly rejected overt religious proclamations, sacraments, and blessings. When Frisch died in 1991, his mourners honored his wishes. Two of Frisch's friends, Peter Bichsel and Michel Seigner, spoke briefly. In closing, Karin Pilliod, Frisch's partner during his final years, read a succinct address he wrote for the gathering: "We let our nearest speak, and without an 'amen.' I am grateful to the ministers of St. Peter's in Zürich . . . for their permission to place the coffin in the church during our memorial service. The ashes will be strewn somewhere." After the abbreviated service, mourners exited to enjoy dinner with a menu Frisch had chosen for them.

Habermas remembered the ceremony as a peculiar event because even though the agnostic Frisch eschewed religious faith, he still intuitively recognized the insufficiency (or "awkwardness," as Habermas put it) of a purely secular funeral. Modernity has provided us with much, but it's mostly at a loss when it comes to dealing with one of the most human and disconcerting mysteries: death.

The story Habermas recounts points to what I've tried to say in many different ways. The church (yes, our community, our people—but also our rituals, our histories, our *institutions*) will not simply fade away or be easily discarded. We may reject her or neglect her, but the church stands witness to something larger than us, something tethered to our primitive memory, something that calls to us in times of distress, at the thresholds of life and death.

As the church, we are the people (whenever we live true to ourselves) who will welcome you into this world, who will join you in marriage and in friendship, who will bless your coming and your going. We will pray for you to prosper and know love's depths even if you think our prayers are foolish or offered in vain, and we will mourn you when you leave us. We will bless the land and the nations we share, and we will grieve together through tragedy and heartache. We will celebrate, with you, everything beautiful and good, everything that comes from the hand of mercy. And then, when your days conclude, we will bury you. We will return you to the earth and pray God's kindness over you.

This is who we are. This is who I hope we will continue to be.

Love big. Be well.
Jonas

A LOVE LETTER

Eastertide / April 2013

Dear Friends,

    Today, I wanted you to know that I love you. It's important to actually say these words. I know I don't say them enough. You are good people, and I'm thankful to be welcomed among you.

Love big. Be well.
Jonas

THE SHYNESS OF GOD

Ordinary Time (Pentecost) / June 2013

Dear Friends,

For those of you who missed last Sunday, Hank Pierce told us part of his story. Though I never met him, most of you remember Hank's dad, James Pierce. Hank began by saying he only remembered his dad laughing outright twice in his life. The first time was when the state surveyor came to map out some of the Pierce land for the highway expansion and got his shiny Chevrolet bogged down in a muddy cow pasture—and by the time he slogged his way back to the road to wave down help, he was covered head to toe in muck and cow dung. The second time James laughed was when, after a long dry spell, he finally bested Hank's mother in a game of dominoes.

"Dad was a serious, uncomplicated man," Hank said, going on to explain how his dad believed in love of God and family, devotion to the land, and a loyalty to the Democratic Party. None of these were laughing matters. And James never once wavered in his certainty about the rightness of any of these commitments. "They were self-evident truths," Hank said, "as unassailable as the fact that sausage comes from pigs."

Given this, you can see why Hank had been afraid to tell his dad, during a weekend break from college, that he was no longer sure he believed in God. After he helped his dad with morning chores, the two sat at the kitchen table with big cups of coffee. With great trepidation, Hank told his dad what he was pondering and the opinions he had begun to form. "I couldn't look Dad in the eye," Hank recalled. "I didn't know whether his response would be fury or sadness, but either way, I didn't want to see it."

After a moment or two, James drew a deep breath. "Well, that's a lot to carry, Hank. How long have you felt this way?"

"I'm not sure," Hank answered. "Maybe a year."

James sighed gently, as if he were releasing some pain from his body. Then he drained the bottom of his cup. "Well, I guess you know most everything I would say to you, right?"

Hank couldn't hold back the grin. "Yes, I think I do."

"Alright, then. Well, I love you. I love you no matter what you believe."

Hank said the great heaviness and darkness he'd been carrying fell off him, like a thick winter coat in spring.

Hank went on to say that there were many things that allowed him to recover faith—or maybe allowed faith to recover him. But he's certain that conversation with his dad, the gentleness and lack of fear his father showed him, proved to be the foundation. James didn't back away or hedge his love; he gave Hank the space he needed. His father's few words and his tenderness let Hank know that his dad was not afraid—and that Hank didn't need to be afraid, either.

"Though my return was long and arduous," Hank told us, "that was the moment I began to believe that maybe the story was true, maybe love really does hold us together."

In contrast to James and the quiet love he showed his son, we Christians often feel anguished by—and compelled to swiftly answer—every doubt that any person struggling with faith voices, any challenge a scientist, philosopher, or ethicist presents. We're terrified that these runaway questions will deliver faith a lethal blow if left unchecked. Unlike us, Jesus didn't lose any sleep over trying to convince people of anything. He simply said, "Here I am. Here's life. Do you want it?"

I know—pastors can be the worst. We get antsy whenever someone strays outside the acceptable boundaries, whenever someone doesn't play along with our agenda. I'm not saying good theology isn't important. What we believe has profound implications for our lives. But good theology tells me that God is in charge, and it's not my job to twist people's arms or guilt them into my way of understanding God and God's world.

Still, Alli would be the first to tell you how often I've gotten myself tied up in all kinds of knots over some of the less-than-stellar choices our kids have made. During an especially dramatic, anxious season with one of our sons (who will not be named here), Alli got me alone after one discussion-turned-blowup. "It's hard enough being a dad," she reminded me. "Don't tackle trying to be God too."

Ever since Hank told us about his conversation with his dad, I've been thinking of God's humility, the patience, the wooing. I'm pondering how Jesus lived (as Chesterton says) with a kind of shyness. Consider Jesus's quiet, tender waiting, exhibiting immense confidence in the good end, the ultimate triumph of God's love. Think of Jesus's refusal to manipulate or swell with self-righteous anger. So, while it would be true to say that God overwhelms us, I think it's also true to say that God *underwhelms* us.

This might make a difference in how we understand and share our faith. Perhaps we don't need to open our mouths every time a New Atheist publishes a new screed. Maybe we could just read and really listen and discover places where we've oversold our case or where we've been hypocritical or untrue to our beliefs. Maybe we could calm the heck down whenever someone asks challenging or angry questions. Maybe we could just listen and trust that God's love will carry us.

I admit I'm tired and heading out for a vacation soon, so there's a chance that I'm just loony with all this. But then again, maybe I'm on to something.

Love big. Be well.
Jonas

NATIVE TIMBER

Advent / November 2013

Dear Friends,

Well, I'm sure most of you have heard by now that Don's had a downturn. I hate cancer. With Don needing to stick closer to home right now, I've been spending quite a bit of time with him, losing my pennies playing Irish poker and watching hours of college football. One of the added benefits of this time with Don is that I've gotten to know his good friend Bill Devers. Though he's part of the regular crew at Stu's, I had only exchanged a few pleasantries with Bill before this; but between losing hands and afternoons going hoarse over Virginia Tech's lackluster season, I've gathered a good bit of Bill's story.

Bill teaches in the architecture department at the university in Moorestown; and he wrote his Ph.D. dissertation on Gustav Stickley, the Midwest farmer-turned-architect who founded the American Craftsman movement before his design and furniture empire imploded. Bill told me how he finagled his way into the abandoned Stickley factory in upstate New York. He roamed the grounds and riffled through dusty catalogs and filled his Canon DSLR with a pictorial history of the splintered dreams of a visionary man who had been wiped out by a run of very bad luck. Bill's big adventure intrigued me partly because I'm a sucker for forgotten history, but also because the episode felt like espionage. I imagined him under cover of moonlight, slipping through a fence with wire cutters, inching through the open factory yard. "Jonas," he corrected me, "it was two in the afternoon, and I had a key from the realtor."

Bill explained how Stickley maintained scrupulous attention to both materials and intricate workmanship. For his corporate logo, he placed the Flemish line *Als ik Kan* inside a joiner's compass. I'm told the phrase means "to the best of my ability." He preferred lumber cut from native timber and insisted that stains never overpower the wood's subtle grain. When Stickley built his own homestead (Craftsman Farms), he foraged materials from the acreage where the house would stand, milled boards from surrounding chestnut trees, and used stones pulled from the soil. He wanted to build a house "reduced to its simplest form," one that would inhabit, not intrude upon, the local landscape.

At any rate, this background on Stickley explains why, when he heard that Abel Braxton would be building our Eucharistic altar, Bill encouraged Don and me to think about the actual plot of earth we called home. "Northern Pin Oaks and Osage Oranges sit on your church's land," Bill told us. "It'd be a shame to haul in lumber from God-knows-where."

You'll remember how several of us gathered on a Saturday morning, and I exercised my fascination with the chainsaw. We felled two trees, replanting as we went. Then we milled the lumber, and Abel went to work. Now, every Sunday, we receive grace around a table intricately woven into our story, our place. It's true that a church in Seattle could feast at this table, but it's also true that it wouldn't mean nearly as much to them. Particulars matter. Stories matter. Places matter.

What we're doing here in our little community is about as plain as it gets. We're not trying to manufacture an idyllic life or an idyllic church. We're trying to be friends with one another, to speak to one another as people who have actual names. I think we could do worse than to make that old joiner's compass our church's icon. Whenever someone asked what vision our church follows, what we're making of our vocations and our loves and our friendships and our families, we could say, "We're making something beautiful, to the best of our ability."

Because Bill talked about Stickley's work with such passion, he inspired me to find out more. I discovered how much of Stickley's philosophy came from the influence of British intellectual John Ruskin. Ruskin pleaded for a return to home goods made by craft guilds (later called "good citizens' furniture"). He advocated for a craft mentality as more human and more beautiful, where the imperfections and inconsistencies inherent in human labor gave a chair or a table or a stone wall its unique character.

This is true for communities as well as craft. Our imperfections, our quirks and our foibles, actually contribute to our character. Sometimes the rough bumps and scratches we try to smooth out are the very things that make us human, true, and beautiful.

So don't raise your kids the way some expert told you to do it. Don't learn to pray the way you imagine our saints practiced their devotion. Jesus rose from the dead to offer the decisive salvo, but everybody gets their own resurrection.

God's making something beautiful out of you; don't short-circuit that by trying to mimic someone else's beauty. And God's making something beautiful out of *all* of us, together. Let's trust that and let it happen.

Love big. Be well.
Jonas

P.S. I was a little giddy when Bill told me the residential architecture Alli and I have always preferred was Craftsman style. We never knew the name of what we loved before, but there it is. A style meant to inhabit, not to intrude. That's what feels like home.

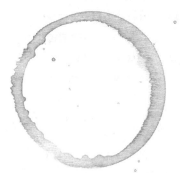

CELEBRITY PREACHERS

Ordinary Time (Epiphany) / February 2014

Dear Friends,

Last week I attended a pastors' convention. I went begrudgingly. I don't care much for Christian conferences in general, but this convention's promotional materials, with the glossy photos of their celebrity lineup, put me in a foul mood. After hearing several of the keynote speakers, I had the impish urge to sling my feet up on the chair in front of me and pull out Annie Dillard or David Sedaris or—heck—*Cosmopolitan*.

In my better moments, I know most of us are simply doing the best we can. Still, all the rah-rah of events like this is just too much for me.

During the grand finale sermon, the speaker concluded with an emotive, stirring story. Almost everyone scooted to the edge of their seats. I know many of these women and men—all pastors who are putting one foot in front of the other, doing the best they know how, expending their sweat and their dreams for the people they love. These folks are tired. Although they find much pleasure and reward in their work, they also endure criticism and put in long hours and wade into deep waters with hurting people. They're not saints, but they pastor mostly with grace. This room of beleaguered souls needed a friend to bring them fresh water and maybe say something like this: *You know, God really loves you. And beaming ear to ear because of the work you're doing. I know that lots of weeks it's tough slogging. Thank you.*

Instead, the speaker stuck to his game plan and pulled the crowd taut, coaxing us into his gripping story set in a poverty-stricken neighborhood. Using a subtle brand of guilt, he prodded us toward action. The story performed to perfection, and you couldn't miss the emotional response rippling through the crowd. The speaker left the stage in triumph. But later I watched the sag of shoulders as my pastoral cohorts and I departed, weary and heavy-hearted. All these speakers had successfully launched their sermons, but they hadn't preached to anybody with a name.

I wonder how many times I've done that to you. How many times have I missed your pain or your joy or your questions and just barged ahead with my theological treatise? How much energy have I exerted trying to "build the church" instead of loving the church—loving *you*? I want to preach sermons that would only fit in Granby. I want to live a life that wouldn't make much sense anywhere else but Granby.

Last November, on the Sunday after news spread about Don's cancer returning, you remember how our prayers took on a life of their own. We were sitting in the quiet, waiting to see if anyone wanted to pray, when Miss Nelson stood up slowly, gripped her walker, and worked her way across the aisle to Don. Then she laid her hands on Don's shoulders and began her slow, earnest prayer. She asked God to take away the cancer, to give the doctors wisdom and "supernatural skill." Eventually she paused, then finished: "Now God, I don't want to tell you how to do your business, but I'm gonna remind you how much we love Don here, how much we need him with us."

As Miss Nelson returned to her pew, most of us were wiping our eyes. I was supposed to deliver the homily next, but even a knucklehead like me could sense how imperceptive it would be to launch into a text when we were sharing such a holy presence. I stood at the pulpit for a moment or two and then closed my Bible. In the silence, Miss Nelson spoke up. "I think we should all gather around Don for a few minutes." And we did. We circled up and hugged Don, more than a few of us sniffling and brushing away tears. It was beautiful.

The next morning at Stu's, Luther said, "Jonas, I believe that's the best sermon I've heard you preach."

Thank God for Miss Nelson. I could have used some of that holiness and humanness at the conference last week. Instead, folks were too busy stepping up to center stage. I'm glad to be back home.

Love big. Be well.
Jonas

AN APOLOGY

Ordinary Time (Epiphany) / February 2014

Dear Friends,

After my last letter, Alli shared a few concerns about it. She said I sounded snarky and used the term "self-serving." Commenting on my vent about church conventions, Amy noted a subtle uptick in my critical bent. Hank, chuckling, dropped off a copy of *Cosmopolitan* with a note taped to the front: *For your next clergy conference*. So my disparagements of other kinds of Christians hadn't gone unnoticed. And Alli didn't mince words when she delivered her final opinion. "It's really not attractive," she told me.

Alli also asked me why I've been preaching angry. I balked at her question, but it's true. I *have* been angry. That's partly because I'm tired. But it's more than that. I'm reacting to my past, to Christians who embarrass me or exhaust me. I'm living out of old stories. I'm often fighting to be true to who I am here and now. After my struggles at our last church, my years spent out of pastoral ministry, and the ways I've changed in response, I've discovered that I'm *persona non grata* in many places where I once thought I belonged. The truth is, my ego has taken a hit, and I've reacted with cynicism and a simmering ugliness.

I wanted to write and say I'm sorry. I want better, for you and for me. Please pray for me.

Love big. Be well.
Jonas

FRIENDSHIP

Eastertide / May 2014

Dear Friends,

From time to time it's important to check to see if the direction we're heading bears any semblance to the course we intended. We don't want to abandon our life simply because we're not paying attention. So most of you know that several months ago our church's governing body, the Session, began evaluating core questions: *Who are we? What are we supposed to be doing? Are we doing the things we're supposed to be doing?* These are important questions—and they aren't only questions for the church. Every few months, Alli and I find it necessary to schedule conversations about our marital state-of-the-union.

Still, at the meeting when the Session decided to engage this process, I apparently exhaled a groan. Luther frowned. "You alright, Jonas?" After I mumbled a lame excuse, the meeting resumed. I know it's unfair for me to download my past story into our current circumstances, but it would be helpful for you to know that at the last church I served, we spent eleven months talking in circles, only to arrive at a document displaying a half-page vision statement followed by long, excursive explanations of twenty-seven church values. *Twenty-seven*. Most of these ideals were noble and defensible, but, taken together, they were suffocating.

Three months later, not a single person in our church could name even half the values, much less actually *value* them. The day I resigned, the conversation with several leaders turned acrimonious. I'm not proud of it, but my motor ran too hot. I pulled out the thick bound report, the result of all those months and all that work. Then I dropped the tome on the table in front of me with a loud thud. "This," I said, "is a year I'll never get back."

So two months ago our Session covered the whiteboard in the manse with an impressive theological vocabulary, boldly written in red, green, and blue. After several energetic hours, we put down our pens and surveyed the scribbled potpourri. We had done good work, but I felt no relief or excitement.

A few of us kept staring at the board. A few of us doodled on our notepads. The silence was finally interrupted by Amy Quitman. "You know, I don't see *friendship* listed anywhere here. It seems to me we could scratch out most of what we've got and just say *friendship*." I sat upright. I think I even laughed. "Yes!" I said. "That's right." I would have given Amy a big kiss on the cheek if I'd thought of it.

In all my years attending the church and serving the church, I had never before heard anyone say, *Hey, you know what we're about? Friendship.* This is remarkable, since Jesus himself gave us the model of his own friendship with us to function as our guide: "My command is this: Love each other as I have loved you. Greater love has no one than this, that he lay down his life for his friends." The next time I find myself among a group of pastors debating the atonement and the precise rationale for Jesus's death, I'm going to say, "Jesus died because he's our friend." I like that. And it's the beating heart of what we believe.

It's the current rage to talk about creating community and being missional and pursuing incarnational ministry, but these well-intentioned notions somehow morph into lofty ideals or complicated strategies that inhibit us from simply *being* friends, *being* neighbors. Even our language betrays us. In church parlance it's common to say that we need to build community, as if true community has a blueprint and a supply list and a timeline for completion. But we do not *build* friendship. We *seek* friendship. We *desire* and *pray for* friendship. We *become* a friend, and then we hope the other will become a friend to us as well. We cannot demand this or maneuver to secure it. We can only walk toward friendship and be grateful for whatever kindness God grants us.

What if we thought of ourselves in simpler terms: friends together in the Kingdom of God. We'd have much more patience with one another. We'd give each other a break. We'd follow Jesus's words in his sermon on the mount: *Be easy on people*. We'd laugh more often. We'd have plenty of gentle space for people to move among us without our clinging to them or expecting them to fill some role for us or for our church. Nothing would be at stake. When I'm with a true friend, I'm free to ponder out loud, to both wonder and wander, to head in the wrong direction, to be foolish—because love sustains us. A true friend finds the good in us when all we see is the mess we've made or the shame heaped upon us. Many of you have helped make Granby a place of friendship for me. Thank you for this rare gift.

Well, as you can tell by now, Amy lit a fire under me that day. With that single word, she explained much of what I believe, and much of what has worn me into the ground.

I've shared how I admire (and am a tad jealous of) the Order of the Roasted Bean at Stu's, those five or six folks who meet most weekdays for breakfast.

Though I've kept giving Amy hints about getting me an invite, she's ignored my clumsy advances. For thirty-two years now, that cadre of friends has shared their coffee, shared their news, and (as they've told me) celebrated retirements, graduations, and grandkids. They've stood beside one another at funerals and during sickness and divorce. They've showed up, morning after morning, through the tedious rigors that fill our lives. They don't harangue each other into participating, and they don't try too hard to define what they've got. And they don't always get along, either—I know, because I've overheard some of their heated exchanges during election season—it gets exciting. Still, they just keep showing up for one another, as often as they're able.

Last month, I noticed a new couple had joined the circle, a man and a woman in their sixties. One of the old-timers pulled two more seats to the table. The conversation proved lively, as always, but now fresh voices joined the familiar ones. What would it feel like to be invited into that tightly knit group, one with such a long, rich history? How powerful it must have been for those two to have someone point to the chairs and say, "Welcome. These are for you." We could learn a lot from that breakfast circle.

Love big. Be well.
Jonas

THE WOUND

Ordinary Time (Pentecost) / September 2014

Dear Friends,

Over the past few weeks I've had several unsettling conversations with some of you, and I believe it's important for all of us to enter these uncomfortable places together. I often hear from many of you how thankful you are to have Luther as chair of our church's Session. Luther has guided us, with much grace and good humor, through several challenging decisions. In our Session, we often hear Luther say, "It's my job to bring the agenda, not the answers." This may be true, but Luther *does* have a real knack for getting the right people around the table so we can at least figure out the next step forward.

Given my admiration for Luther and our church's gratitude for his leadership, I was shocked when he told me several weeks ago how he feels more and more on the periphery of our community. This needling awareness became heightened for him over recent months (years, really) because our country has endured fresh racial wounds.

Most of us have not known what to say or how to respond, and I realize now how our silence (*my silence too*) has only pressed into these wounds, only compounded the isolation and the pain.

I know you love Luther, Glynna, and their kids, as I do. So I asked Luther to write to you, to tell us all what's been weighing on him so heavily. His letter is attached. I trust you will receive it with the generous spirit Luther has always demonstrated toward our entire community—a generosity that, I now understand, has cost him more than I ever imagined.

Love big. Be well.
Jonas

LUTHER'S LETTER

Dear Community of Granby Pres,

When Jonas asked me to write this letter, my immediate response was no. I resisted for two reasons. First, it seems strange and out of place to put all this down on paper for you to read by yourself. Over the years, whenever we've had issues in our church, we've always talked things through eye to eye, and I believe that's the best way. And second (and more on this in a moment), I'm tired of being the spokesperson for the black community. I'm one person. I'm *me*. I don't want to represent anything or anyone other than myself.

But as I thought more about Jonas's request, it occurred to me that if I stayed quiet, something inside me would recede. And that's why I changed my mind. I love this church, and our friendships here mean a great deal to me. Maybe there's no good way to go about something like this. Maybe this is one of those occasions where we simply have to dive in.

Let me be clear. I'm not angry or wanting some quick fix for what I'm about to share, but I *do* need to be honest. As the only black family in the congregation, my family has felt an awkwardness, or maybe a detachment, more often than I wish were true. On the first Sunday we visited, so many years ago, I thought I might drown in all the whiteness. But everyone was so welcoming, and another family invited us out to lunch. So we just kept coming back. We have never doubted that you wanted us here or that your arms were open to us. Please don't hear anything I say as a lack of gratitude for the genuine friendships we have or as any broad-brush tainting of the legitimate community we share. But if our friendships are ever to deepen and if our community is to be a true and honest one, there are things I now know I must say.

Whenever racial issues arise in our neighborhood—or when the horrific stories hit the news like they have with such force lately—I notice how some of you tiptoe around me, never broaching the subject I know all of us are talking about—only not with each other. This silent barrier increases my sense of isolation. I know that many of you are afraid of saying the wrong thing, and I understand that our views on racial problems and their remedies are complicated and uncomfortable. But when no one ever says anything and we just avoid the topic, that silence speaks volumes. Are we more committed to a superficial peace than we are to actually being *for* each other, *with* each other?

On the other hand, sometimes some of you do come to me and ask the kind of questions that make me feel like I'm expected to be a stand-in for every black person in America. As I said at the start of this letter, I don't speak for black people. I speak for *me*. I don't know how to navigate this issue, and my two competing frustrations offer little clarity on what I'm asking from you. I guess I'm just asking you to be our friends. I want you to be okay with discomfort. I want you to ask hard questions—but I want you to ask your questions in an effort to understand me, not to understand "the black community."

And yet, of course, I am part of the black community (among other communities), and I do get angry when the chronic injustices of America's racial sin seem lost on some who I consider my dearest friends. When the riot broke out in Ferguson, it was hard to hear all the disgust over the violence (a violence I too detest) with no equal indignation over the long history of despair giving birth to this outrage and chaos. This stuff doesn't combust overnight. It's the boiling over of a long simmer, the fruit of old and pernicious evils. This stuff isn't simply the result of a few rogue police officers or a handful of criminals hitting the streets.

These communities (and I know—I grew up in a rough section of Baltimore) buckle under the decades-long strain of antagonistic law enforcement (not all but enough bad apples to make a mark), judicial double standards, schools limping along with bare-to-the-bone budgets. Does it seem right to you that young black men are routinely tossed into jail for months at a time over a little bit of weed (leaving their children and their mothers to fend for themselves), while white-collar criminals, who surely harm more people, regularly get off with a minimal fine? No wonder so many in these communities feel enraged or hopeless. There's no excuse for anyone acting the fool, but can you understand how it's a powder keg waiting to explode? Can you feel their pain? I do. I've felt it up close.

The toughest prejudice to root out is the prejudice we refuse to believe exists. We don't have plantations anymore, of course, and we do have affirmative action and civil rights legislation. But institutional and social systems sustain a racism that continued long after slavery, making it something like a rigged Monopoly game. For generations, blacks were restrained while whites circled the board a hundred times. And then, after all the property was bought up, we were given permission to join the game. Black communities may have the same "rights" white communities have, but the resources, the power structures, the intangible knowledge and accumulated wealth and societal infrastructure built over hundreds of years—that's something blacks can't conjure with the wave of a wand or the passing of a law. I don't know what to do about this, and I know I risk fracturing friendships by speaking this frankly. But I want, I *need* you to understand the displacement I feel.

Sometimes I think my family's presence too easily relieves the pressure of difficult conversations, as if having a black family in our congregation proves that no one here is racist. But I don't want our church to point to me as proof that racial issues are no longer our problem. They *are* our problem; they're just buried deep. And if I may be blunt, I can't carry the burden of being your one black friend who must constantly explain how and why racism exists. Playing that part is lonely and fatiguing. I just can't do it.

Racism is a deep wound that bleeds into our own history. Did you know that the lot where our church sits was part of several large tracts of land stolen from blacks across this region through peonage (a version of sharecropping rightly referred to as "debt slavery")? Did you know that Mr. Nellie Johnson, the grocer, was denied the GI Bill after he returned from the War? Mr. Nellie had a Purple

Heart, but the Jim Crow administrators did what they did so often—they discovered loopholes to deny him education funding because he was black. Reports show that this kind of discrimination was widespread. So Mr. Nellie never went to university. Did you know our state's housing authority maneuvered land zoning so as to effectively cut out blacks from having access to government-backed mortgages? And these are the same educational opportunities and the same mortgages that economists say built the white middle class.

So how do we make up for all these injustices? How do we make things right? Can you understand why simply lecturing folks in Ferguson about not getting violent makes someone like me feel angry or hopeless?

I know some of us say we'd like our church to better reflect the racial and socio-economic mosaic of God's Kingdom. I don't know any better than you how to make this happen. I don't know if more color on Sunday morning is even the right goal. Our family is here because we love you and we know you love us, and I'm trusting that love a whole lot with this letter. I've raised more questions than solutions, but in the end this is not a problem to be solved. I really just want you to see all of me, to know these painful things. I want our conversations to be open even when we're talking about the hard stuff. I want to believe our relationships are strong enough for us to find the healing that I'm now realizing I've looked for my entire life. I hope and pray we will find this healing together.

I expect my letter will raise lots of questions. Some of you will disagree with how I see things. But I won't be bothered by that. My prayer is that this letter allows us to get everything on the table so we can talk freely and honestly at last.

Sincerely,
Luther DuBois

HOPE

Ordinary Time (Pentecost) / September 2014

Dear Friends,

Since Luther's letter reached us, we've shared numerous difficult conversations. Anxiety has flared a few times, and we've had to work hard to stop and listen to one another. I'm so thankful for Luther's courage—and for the courage of so many of you who have committed to step into these uncomfortable places. I think our response has been a corrective to previous discussions with our Session around diversity in our church. *Diversity* is a word, but Luther is our *friend*. When we're standing by each other in these places of discomfort—these are precisely the moments when our commitments to one another have to do the heavy lifting.

Let's keep at it. All this has challenged me in ways I'd prefer to ignore, but ultimately I'm grateful for the discomfort. I have a lot of hope for where I think we're heading.

Love big. Be well.
Jonas

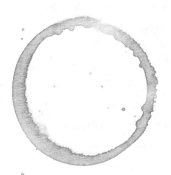

A LIFETIME OF DROWNING

Advent / November 2014

Dear Friends,

This morning, on the way out my back door,
I paused for another sad look at my frostbitten
heirloom tomatoes. The Cherokee Purples I planted
last spring yielded a grand total of five inedible,
marble-sized buds. Maybe you'll remember how I
shared my initial enthusiasm for them in a sermon,
how I researched varietals, how I peppered Eva
at the farmer's market with questions and fussed
over the soil every bit as much as Hank fusses over
his chili at our annual cook-off. In the sermon, I
labored to connect these seeds planted in hope
with the mysteries of grace and the ripe, overflow-
ing bushels sure to come. Here's one of the many
reasons a preacher shouldn't offer a story—or a
sermon—before its time.

This morning, as I paused over the death of my
dream, I thought of a conversation with a parish-

ioner years ago. This woman had been taking life on the chin, deep and painful disappointment. When we spoke, a flash of fire ignited in her eyes. "I expected God to make things go better," she told me. "I didn't sign up for this."

"Actually, you did," I answered, without calibrating for appropriate empathy.

She bristled. "What?"

"Were you baptized?"

"Yes," she answered.

"Well, then you signed up for exactly this."

That may not have been my best moment of pastoral compassion or wise timing, but what I said is true. Our baptismal vows speak of new life, but they speak of death first. When you go under, you're not getting some light splash to rinse off the dust. No—you drown under those murky waters. I've always thought we pull people back to the surface too fast. A person could get whiplash from our rush to get past the dying. In the baptismal rite, after I say "in the name of the Father, the Son, and the Holy Spirit" and right before I push someone under, I'd like to add these words: *Now take a big breath and hold tight—this is going to take a minute.* If I were able to be baptized again, I'd want to come up gasping for air, my senses shocked raw by the rush of oxygen, jolted by the grace that brought me back from the brink.

You've probably picked up on my strange relationship with infant baptism. It's a mysterious grace, I'll grant you. But I think something's missed when a body doesn't experience the helpless sensation of drowning in the water, only to be rescued by strong hands in the nick of time. So if we do baptize our babies, I'm all for the dunking, even with them. None of this safe and sterile dabbing of water on the forehead. Submerge those dear children in the love of Jesus—God knows they'll need it. They'll come up confused and squalling, but that seems about right to me. All of us should know the gift of such a disorienting encounter with love.

A few months ago, little June Dixon was taking part in our confirmation class, preparing for her baptism. She peppered her dad with questions after my talk of baptism and death and coming back to life. One afternoon on the car ride home, she stared out the window and chewed at her lip. "Dad, does it hurt?"

"Does what hurt, honey?" Jack asked.

"Does it hurt when you die and when you come back to living?"

Jack handled the situation deftly and with great gentleness, as we all expect he would. But I'll say this: June understood better than most of us.

Baptism happens to us once, but it prepares us for a lifetime of drowning, a lifetime of being rescued. Baptism teaches us that we really can sink into deep waters. We can lay down our bodies, and along with our bodies, we can relinquish our fears and our strivings, our demands and our restlessness. We can lay down our anxieties over what we do not know and what we cannot control, our terror at being discovered as a fraud—we can lay it all down. We really can drown. It's okay. It will be okay. Love will be enough to hold us.

Maybe Jesus made baptism central to our faith for this simple reason: to believe in God is to believe that love is sufficient to hold us. Jesus came so we could live well, but we have to learn to die well first.

Do you remember when Don Brady was baptized six years ago? It was memorable for everything that happened that day, but also because it was my first baptism at Granby. I thought about this story while preparing for Don's funeral last month. Don was such a herculean man, wasn't he? He came to faith at age fifty-six, after his initial diagnosis and remission but years before cancer finally took him. I remember it was February and bone-chilling cold, but he didn't want to wait a single moment for his baptism. So I arranged for us to borrow First Baptist's baptistery, since the Baptists have the good sense to offer heated options for bitter winters. When I told Don our plan, he would have none of it. "I want the full Monty," he said. "Jesus didn't get dunked in some tub."

I'm sure you've at least heard the story of Don's

baptism because it's now canonized in our church's folklore. It was February 29, thirty-nine degrees, two days after an epic blizzard. Copper Run River was frigid, so icy the poor fish were floating there limp, like they'd been Tasered. The wind was blistering, and most of you were absolutely incredulous that we were participating in such foolishness.

Only a handful of us made our way down to the water. Don wore the traditional white robe, but what you don't know is that Don didn't wear a stitch of clothes underneath. I had on long johns and waders, but he wore nothing but this thin sheet. When we were dressing in my office, I noticed him pulling the flimsy robe over his mammoth, naked body. "Uh, Don, wear your clothes. Just pull the robe over on top. This is going to be brutal."

"Not a chance," Don answered. "I'm going bare as a baby's booty."

"Why would you do that?" I asked.

"I've had death in my bones. I want the forgiveness to get in just as deep."

When we stepped into the water, Don went tense with the shock of cold. His back tightened, and he sucked air through his teeth. "Wowzers," he said. "That'll shrivel a man quick."

We waded in until the water was waist-deep. Don took short breaths, like a mother in labor—but with no grimacing or complaining, only calm.

159

I'd even say he was relaxed. Don was a man at peace, a man who had truly let go. Just before I spoke the solemn words and put him under the water, I asked him if he wanted to say anything. "I'm ready," he whispered. "I've never been more ready. Ain't love grand."

When my frustrated friend told me she expected God to do better by her, she forgot that baptism doesn't promise an escape from death. Instead, it promises that our deaths—of every kind—will not finish us. God's love will hold us up. God's love will, in the end, raise us up. So we can let loose. We can laugh and breathe free. Our life is not ours to hold together.

Love big. Be well.
Jonas

SABBATHS EVERYWHERE

Ordinary Time (Epiphany) / March 2015

Dear Friends,

Before I became your pastor nearly six years ago (can you believe it?), the Session and I met in the manse on the weekend Alli and I visited. I had four questions scribbled on a 3x5 card tucked into my back pocket. Most seminaries list thirty or forty questions they believe every potential pastor should discuss with a congregation. That's probably good advice, but I suffer from a short attention span.

I remember my second question vividly: "What's Granby's policy on pastoral sabbaticals?"

"We insist on them," Amy Quitman answered.

I must have looked stunned or bewildered. "That alright with you?" Amy asked.

"Yes," I said. "Yes, I insist on them too." But the truth was I'd only come to this conviction after leaving ministry. Before, I had always hoped for a sabbatical, but I had never had a Session show this kind of attentiveness to my family or me. I had never been given the gift of church leaders working proactively to help me guard my soul's well-being. I felt such relief (maybe even *safety,* if that makes sense) to find people who wanted their pastor to be something more than the Energizer bunny pounding that blasted bass drum into infinity.

At this point Luther spoke up, explaining how the church was familiar with sabbaticals, given the influence of the university and the academic precedence for a regular sabbatical schedule. Then Hank Pierce waved his hand as if shooing away a fly. "Ah, you don't need any university to know about sabbaticals. Any half-pint gardener knows you've got to rotate the crop and give the dirt a rest."

Hank, as you know, wasn't about to miss the opportunity to preach his sermon. "That's the problem with those humungous farms gobbling up half the county and keeping the operation buzzing 24/7. They don't have the sense to know when to stop. They don't know when enough's enough." Hank leaned back in his chair, gathering steam for his final push. "It's all dollars and donuts now, but sooner or later the dirt'll give up on 'em."

That was the moment I decided we were moving to Granby.

So the general policy for pastors and sabbaticals is this: After every six years, we get six months to step away and take a deep breath, to get a clear head and fresh eyes. The idea is that if God took a break after six days of work, then maybe we should follow his lead. This informs our larger understanding of rhythms and Sabbaths and rest. So, each week a pastor gets a day of Sabbath (in addition to a standard day off—that's different). Each year, a pastor gets a few weeks of Sabbath. And then, every six years, a pastor gets a much longer stretch of time. The hope is that Sabbaths (or sabbaticals) will be part of an ongoing life of rest and work that yields rich fruit. I like the way Walter Brueggemann puts it: "As you know, the creation ends in Sabbath. God is so overrun with fruitfulness that God says, 'I've got to take a break from all this. I've got to get out of the office.'"

Of course, all this sounds tidier than the reality. The fact is I'm sucking wind right now. I do need a break. Still, I feel self-conscious. Not everyone gets to have this stretch of days, and I'm acutely aware of that. Alli and I remain overwhelmed by your generosity toward us, your well wishes for us. A few of you seem almost as excited as we are about our six months in Spain. Thank you for that extraordinary gift.

My greatest hope for our community is that our sabbatical reminds us all that our life is much more than what we accomplish. We really do need tangible ways to resist the insidious idea that we must always be moving, always be working. When I think of so many of you who have no possibility of spending months like this, I feel awkward. I'd love it if my doctor took a sabbatical and then, the next time I was in her office, she saw me with new eyes and rejuvenated insight. I'd love it if the carpenter who's been working on our kitchen took a sabbatical and then returned to his craft with fresh inspiration and newfound joy.

This is why we talk so much about Sabbath. I hope we will all learn how to be a people at rest, a people of Sabbath. We need to rest, to make time for joy. Sabbath looks different for everyone, but if we don't have a regular way to pull the plug and shut down the engines, then we're playing a dangerous game. Perhaps it's possible for a person to exist at breakneck speed, but I'm not sure anyone can truly *live* this way.

Sabbath comes as a gift. Sabbath reminds us it's good to knock off early, to pull down the window shades and do nothing, to dream and ruminate, to waste time, to decline an invitation, to toss energy and money at some craft or art we know will never turn a profit, to play like a child or to play *with* a child. Sabbath tells us it's good and holy to both rest and play, to take pleasure in God's good world, to be free, to leave behind the incessant clamor. Thomas Aquinas's wisdom applies here: *There must be no noise on the Sabbath.*

The cries of lovers are excepted. That sounds about right to me.

When I'm out of rhythm, one of Wendell Berry's poems returns me to this spirit of Sabbath. This will be my prayer for us, and for you, while we're gone:

When despair for the world grows in me
and I wake in the night at the least sound
in fear of what my life and my children's lives may be,
I go and lie down where the wood drake
rests in his beauty on the water, and the great heron
*   feeds.*
I come into the peace of wild things
who do not tax their lives with forethought
of grief. I come into the presence of still water.
And I feel above me the day-blind stars
waiting with their light. For a time
I rest in the grace of the world, and am free.

So, in a few weeks, the McAnns depart for our sabbatical. I pray we find rest these days, and I pray the same for you.

Love big. Be well.
Jonas

AFTER WORDS

APPROPRIATELY, THIS BOOK BEGAN WITH A friend and a letter. Thank you, Amy Walker. And then these pages took shape during a marvelous sabbatical in Colorado. I am grateful for serving a church, All Souls Charlottesville, which provides space for solitude, family, prayer, and creativity.

Thank you, Lil Copan, for sticking with this project for so long; your red pen has an artful sweep. And Mary Hietbrink, you tended this work like a good gardener, pulling weeds and pruning excess—you let the beauty grow free.

My deepest gratitude goes to my best friend, Miska. Our life together runs through every word, every story. And to my sons: Wyatt and Seth, I love you.

Winn Collier
Longdream Cottage
Eastertide 2017